EMOTIONAL INTELLIGENCE

Improve Your Relationships by Raising Your Eq

(How to Develop Your Emotional Intelligence to Have a High Eq)

Barbara Smith

Published by Chris David

Barbara Smith

All Rights Reserved

Emotional Intelligence: Improve Your Relationships by Raising Your Eq (How to Develop Your Emotional Intelligence to Have a High Eq)

ISBN 978-1-77485-337-5

All rights reserved. No part of this guide may be reproduced in any form without permission in writing from the publisher except in the case of brief quotations embodied in critical articles or reviews.

Legal & Disclaimer

The information contained in this book is not designed to replace or take the place of any form of medicine or professional medical advice. The information in this book has been provided for educational and entertainment purposes only.

The information contained in this book has been compiled from sources deemed reliable, and it is accurate to the best of the Author's knowledge; however, the Author cannot guarantee its accuracy and validity and cannot be held liable for any errors or omissions. Changes are periodically made to this book. You must consult your doctor or get professional medical advice before using any of the suggested remedies, techniques, or information in this book.

Upon using the information contained in this book, you agree to hold harmless the Author from and against any damages, costs, and expenses, including any legal fees potentially resulting from the application of any of the information provided by this guide. This disclaimer applies to any damages or injury caused by the use and application, whether directly or indirectly, of any advice or information presented, whether for breach of contract, tort, negligence, personal injury, criminal intent, or under any other cause of action.

You agree to accept all risks of using the information presented inside this book. You need to consult a professional medical practitioner in order to ensure you are both able and healthy enough to participate in this program.

Table of Contents

INTRODUCTION 1

CHAPTER 1: THE FIRST CHAPTER IS ABOUT BECOMING EMOTIONALLY INDEPENDENT 4

CHAPTER 2: WHAT IS THE SCIENCE BEHIND EMOTIONAL INTELLIGENCE 14

CHAPTER 3: YOUR RESPONSES TO OTHERS 21

CHAPTER 4: THE EMOTIONAL SELF-DISCIPLINE 27

CHAPTER 5: KEYS TO SUCCESS TO CONTROLLING YOUR EMOTIONS 35

CHAPTER 6: TESTED TECHNIQUES TO IMPROVE THE EMOTIONAL INTELLIGENCE 42

CHAPTER 7: THE WAYS OF SELF-IMPROVEMENT 49

CHAPTER 8: DETACHMENT IS THE KEY TO A GREAT CONNECTION 63

CHAPTER 9: THE REASONS WHY GAINING EMOTIONAL INTELLIGENCE IS ESSENTIAL 72

CHAPTER 10: PROGRAMMING YOURSELF TO BE SUCCESSFUL 84

CHAPTER 11: THE SLAVE OF THE MACHINE 93

CHAPTER 12: MAINTAIN YOUR PRINCIPLES 98

CHAPTER 13: STAYING INFORMED AND INTERESTED 103

CHAPTER 14: WHAT TO CHANGE YOUR MIND TO NOT BE ANGRY 110

CHAPTER 15: YOGA AND MINDFULNESS MEDITATION .. 131

CHAPTER 16: THE TOPIC IS CONFLICT MANAGEMENT ... 144

CHAPTER 17: THE HABITS TO DEVELOP TO ENSURE SUCCESS 151

CHAPTER 18: BEING AWARE OF YOUR EMOTIONS 166

CONCLUSION 182

Introduction

When we read the title of the book, we might think that the book discusses some deeply Stephen Hawking theories on emotional aptitude as well as the mathematical formulas that form the brain of an emotional intelligent person.

This book is quite unique. It starts by trying to explain the general emotions, and after that, it explains the significance and significance of the term "emotional intelligence. It reveals numerous secrets to be emotionally intelligent. You read it right. Everyone can be emotionally clever.

There's no one who is perfect living. We all are imperfect in our own unique ways, and should be able to be able to accept each other's imperfections. So, there should not be one person who is saying, "Nah man! This book isn't my thing." Why is that? It's because the book an offering to humanity! It not only helps us to recognize our emotions, but also teaches us how to control your emotions prior to them control us.

As you read this book, you'll be able to comprehend what emotion is. It will help you take your emotions into consideration and be able to recognize them. The nature of our bodies to respond so easily and precisely based on each emotion that is expressed is a topic that is often emphasized. We need to learn to discern and comprehend the messages our body is trying to tell us.

We will help you in the process of identifying your emotions, understanding the connection between your behavior and emotions and how to manage them , and then how to harness them to be your advantage. There is a great connection between our feelings and how we behave. This book explains in detail on the foundations and methods for controlling your emotions as well as your actions.

To be emotionally smart, you must to be able to recognize and comprehend your own emotions as well as the emotions of those who are around you. In order to achieve this you need to be confident and self-aware, as well as possess self-control. This book will help you to achieve this. all your questions about these three components will be answered : which ones they're, what's the best way you can achieve them, how to keep them, and the best way to develop a lasting emotional intelligence with these three elements.

When you get to the final chapter the book you'll know how to overcome your personal weaknesses and put yourself on the right path towards success.

Chapter 1: The first chapter is about becoming emotionally Independent

When you have completed the exercises in chapter 2 to help you to be more connected to your emotions, you've probably discovered that things aren't always exactly as it ought to be. The focus on your emotional state is already giving an understanding of the way these emotions affect your reactions and behavior.

You may have noticed that your behavior shifts positively when you experience positive emotions. You may also have discovered the ways you deal with those negative emotion (primary as well as secondary) and learnt to identify the mechanisms that allow them. Knowing this may have given you the ability to modify your response in response to negative emotions. This also provided you with an benefit in your interactions with others at home and in your professional life.

It's easy to imagine how these skills can affect your relationships with your colleagues, friends as well as your boss. When you review your emotions and feelings you might notice that certain circumstances can create obstacles for you to attain a greater level of emotional intelligence which will further enhance the quality of your interpersonal relationships and increase your chances of success and happiness. Even if this didn't happen, there's always opportunities to improve.

It is crucial to understand the influence of other people on our feelings. For instance, a speedy driver may cause us to feel angry, or even fearful about our lives. Similar situations are commonplace in everyday daily lives. Our moods depend, in a large degree, influenced by the actions and feelings of others, which can make us feel depressed and feeling powerless. It's time to put an end to the cycle. It's time to become emotionally free.

Understanding and defining emotional dependence

Emotional dependency is when you allow someone else to influence your feelings and feelings. The majority of the time, this type of emotional dependence can be observed in relationships with a romantic partner in which one person becomes dependent on another spouse's moods and behaviors. If, for instance, someone is feeling unhappy for reasons that they cannot identify the reason, they may begin searching for a way to ease the sadness by involving their partner. This is typically connected to feelings of emptyness within which they believe that the other person will help fill.

The reason behind this could be traced back to the fact that this person is unable to interpret or recognize their own emotional state effectively and is seeking someone who can. Another reason why this could happen is because the individual isn't aware of how to express a certain emotion (for instance, the feeling of love) and is relying on their partner to bring the desired emotion.

The process typically involves surrendering control of your emotions and then transferring them to other people. Although this may appear to be an easy way to escape personal responsibility, it could affect one's self-esteem negatively, which could further hinder the capacity to socially interact and establish healthy relationships.

In a larger sense, emotional dependence is the inability to escape completely from others' emotions to ensure your own emotional well-being. Being mindful of your emotional well-being is preventing the reckless driver to irritate you by his reckless behaviour (which is likely motivated by his own emotions).

But, the sensation of fear that comes with the incident of a reckless driver could be a lifesaver. If the driver got closer to us or if we were not able to clear the way, the vehicle could strike us. Our immediate emotional reaction (of being scared) could cause us to enter fighting or flight mode in which we (most people) would attempt to leap away from the vehicle. In this scenario the fear caused by another individual can be beneficial and helpful.

In this manner, emotional dependence can be an unwieldy weapon. It is crucial to be emotionally secure by remaining in control over your feelings. Through emotional independence that you can fully realize your potential in emotional intelligence and perform at your top in business, social or romantic relationships.

But, complete separation from the world could stop you from being able to discern the emotions of others and cause you to be unable to make connections with other people. There are methods that can assist you in find the perfect balance between emotional dependence and emotional independence , so you can make the right choice between both.

Refusing to believe in unhelpful thinking

An approach that is practical is required in addressing thoughts that are not helpful, but also maintaining an appropriate level of emotional dependence that allows us to develop our emotional intelligence. The best method to achieve this is to alter the patterns of thought or behaviors that cause your struggles. Through changing your habits and thoughts it is possible to change how you feel.

If you do this you will be able to manage psychological, emotional, and cognitive issues that hinder you from truly connecting with your self. This will enable you to develop an emotional self-reliance that is not influenced by the negative feelings that are a part of your life.

Being in the presence of the emotional influence of others could drag you down to a state of emotional discord that can alter your perspective of your own self and other people. This could lead to being entrapped within negative thoughts. Ideas such as "I have to be bad since I wasn't capable of restraining the external influences, isn't it?"

Wrong! This is precisely the kind of thinking you should confront. It's not going to help you in any way. It actually robs you of the chance to improve yourself as a person and show yourself in the most professional possible manner. It can cause unhealthy feelings that lead to self-destructive behaviors.

1) Disputing (Duration 1 - 2 weeks)

Disputing is an exercise to help you confront the irrational and unhealthy thinking. You can improve your reasoning and lessen your belief systems that are not rational through this exercise for at minimum ten minutes each day. You'll begin to see some improvements within the first couple of days. For a more lasting impact, you may consider incorporating it into your routine for at minimum 3-4 weeks. Begin by asking yourself the following questions:

1.) Which self-defeating negative ideas do I need to eliminate?

2) What particulars is this negative idea based on?

3) What other evidence do you have to prove that this notion is untrue (or at the very least exaggerated)?

4) What is the most terrible possible outcome for me if this theory turns into a fact?

5) What is the most beneficial possible outcome for me should this belief turn out to be untrue?

These questions can help you identify and comprehend the negative thinking. Additionally, they can help you cope with situations that lead to automatic and involuntary emotional dependence. Through regular exercise, you'll be able to recognize the moment this type of thinking is developing and then change it into positive and healthier thinking. After a few days your responses to these questions might appear like this:

1.) My character is a sham, and nobody loves me.

2) I had a major dispute in a fight with my partner.

3) I am blessed with a husband who is a true friend who shows his love for me each day through random gestures of love.

4) I remain a bad person , and nobody would ever love me. If this is the case that nothing will alter much.

5) I am beginning to realize that I'm not a bad person , and people actually like me. This means I'm not a bad guy and people do like me.

It is possible to use these questions to help you deal with various situations and negative thoughts you may observe within your own mind. Once you've been through this, it becomes automatic and you'll be able to stop these kinds of thoughts in a flash. Imagine the amount you would achieve if you were to avoid the temptation of letting another's mood lead you to begin thinking this way.

In the first place you'll be able to demonstrate to the other person that you're strong and independent. Furthermore, this ability to overcome negative thinking can help you manage high tension and stressful situations. This means that you'll be able to act more effectively under stress. However, this is only the beginning. The skills and knowledge that you've acquired about managing and controlling your emotions can help you comprehend the those around you throughout the day.

Chapter 2: What is the Science Behind Emotional Intelligence

In the beginning, I'd like introduce you to the prefrontal cortex (frontal lobes) as the planning and processing centre. It is the principal brain region that is connected with analytical thinking, intelligence as well as problem-solving, personal growth and development.

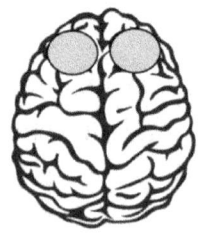

Then, we get the archipallium, also known as primitive brain. The archipallium is directly connected with the stem of your brain, and is responsible for your fundamental activities like breathing, sleep, and food digestion.

The amygdala, which is a part of the brain that manages memory and regulates emotional responses.

This tiny area can detect threats to our physical and emotional well-being and triggers stomach reactions as well as an emotional response known as the Triple F reflex (fight, freeze or flight). Depression, anxiety, and anger are all emotions that trigger the Amygdala when it senses threats, with all these responses intended to shield our bodies from danger.

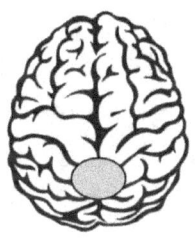

To give a real-life example take a trip back to the beginning of man's time, when threats might be in the form of predators that ate meat.

When predators were identified, the amygdala recognized the predator as an imminent threat. The amygdala's signals would trigger the release of adrenalin and a rise in heart rate. The body felt nervous as muscles prepared to go into action, and the instinct of the gut kicked into action to flee, fight or even freeze.

Today, we are in the midst of a crisis and our amygdala keeps responding to threats, but that most threats stem from our thoughts. The response to threats is actually the result of stress. There's only a limit to how many things the human brain is able to handle until it has to recharge. One common analogy could be the stress Sieve. The brain inside us is the equivalent of a sieve. The amygdala also connects directly to this when it senses dangers and then fires.

Let's look at it a bit closer.

Visualize your motivational energy throughout the day like water in the balloon. Each event that causes stress and causes your amygdala to ignite is a pin that pokes into the balloon, so that the water begins to drip out. The alarm clock does not go off, the milk spills across the floor during the hurry to get dressed for work, there's an inordinate amount of traffic during the commute to work and there aren't any parking spaces at the parking lot. It is evident how fast the pins pricks inside the balloon begin to pile to.

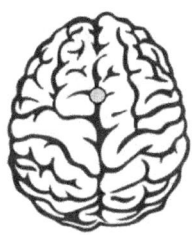

The level of water (mental energy) decreases inside the balloon, the same goes for your capability to manage incoming situations effectively as your brain tries to manage and recover from every event.

However, there is an ability to replenish the levels of water. This is achieved through the process of relaxation and rest. Our body recuperates while we rest But what's a bit most people are not aware of is that the brain active during this time processing the information of the day's events and also repairing itself.

Imagine your mind as a huge office.

In the course of the day, thoughts come as papers that go into the in tray. Desk papers get scattered around as we search for memories and map the thoughts that are required to work and at home. As we lie down the organizer arrives for the evening shift and starts to sort documents, making notes, and creating the memory board, leaving everything clean for the following day.

Naturally, your brain is capable of doing much more than that however you'll see the idea. When we relax and do things that make us content and at the same time, during our time off it allows the levels of water in our balloons to have time to replenish.

It is a fact that rest time is equally important for mental healing as physical recovery.

Chapter 3: Your Responses to Others

What are your reactions when people make mistakes? If you are impatient it is important to realize that there are reasons for these errors. People who are emotionally intelligent are able to put themselves in the other's shoes and demonstrate compassion. Empathy is essential in every relationship. It's more than just thinking about how the other person's feelings are like. It's about looking at the way that person is feeling about the error made. A lot of times you'll see the people who learn from their mistakes and making a big amount of them doesn't accomplish any good. But staying calm and talking about the issue with someone else can alter their perspective completely and teach how to approach issues from a different angle the next time.

Things to watch out for when you are trying to determine your capacity to apply emotional intelligence to others include:

* Do you use active listening?

* Are you compassionate?

* Are you compassionate?

Are you afraid to admit guilt?

Are you able to assist others and show them praise?

A person who is emotionally intelligent can demonstrate these capabilities and be able to listen to others while defending their own interests from an emotional perspective. Listening allows you to comprehend more however active listening is more than it. You can discern through the body language of others what they are saying and better discern through the lines. This puts you in a better position than someone more eager to voice his own views and not pay attention to what's being stated. If you talk to business owners who are successful, you'll find that active listening is an integral role to their accomplishment. They hire people who can do what they do and, as they pay them lots of money to perform the work, they recognize they need to listen to the concerns is a smart method to improve their performance.

Another aspect that people often don't associate with emotional intelligence , is their capacity to make amends. The majority of people hold to their opinions and don't want to acknowledge when they're believed to have committed an error. This isn't smart in any way, since when you make an apology you can let the issue go and move on to the next. The ability to forgive is also an essential part of being emotionally competent. Find a way to work it out. If you have grudges with somebody, then who suffers? It is important to realize that the pain happens inside your head, not within the head of the culprit, therefore it is not a good idea to blame someone else. It is much more sensible to realize that mistakes were made and to quickly accept forgiveness because it frees the emotional baggage. Let me provide you with an example.

Kirsty can't forgive her ex-husband because of his infidelity. The actions he took, she considers inexplicably wrong. She is carrying around the negative feelings that her experience has caused her to be weighed down and, when she encounters individuals she meets for the first time, she immediately is suspicious of them as untrustworthy. She is therefore cautious about things that haven't yet transpired. Helen however, on her other hand, discovered that her husband had a tendency to stray because he was unsure of his masculinity.

While the act of unfaithfulness is a source of disgust for her, she's not ready to enter into new relationships with the assumption that they will be not trustworthy. She is sane and recognizes there's two aspects to any story. Because she does not hold an opinion, she is in a position to begin new relationships as a complete person instead of storing the emotional baggage as a weapon to defend herself. Of the two of them, Helen is more likely to enter an unrelated partnership with her head up due to the fact that Kirsty brings all of her negative baggage and reveals herself to be insufficient before the relationship has been able to begin or even begin.

Your attitude towards other people's actions affect how you think. If you're able to forgive, then you do not need to be a victim. If you can be compassionate towards others, you will be better able to view the world from different perspectives and understand that everyone has the right to express their own opinion. That means you are more likely to acquire knowledge as you're able to pay attention to new ideas and make decisions on your own which ones are pertinent to your personal life and which ones aren't, and while being respectful enough to recognize that each person has their own perspective on life.

You can enhance your interpersonal abilities by learning to speak in a clear manner. Examine how you respond to others and work on areas in which you display any signs of weakness and you'll increase your emotional intelligence immediately. You'll earn respect from others and be respected by them This is the essence of what emotional intelligence is about.

Chapter 4: The Emotional Self-Discipline

The most crucial aspect that students learn at the school? What aspect is more important than homework or textbooks? What aspect of your life can make you more confident and is felt when it is not?

It's self-control!

What's discipline to relate to emotional intelligence? Great question! The best method to answer it is to consider asking yourself whether you can apply the techniques in the preceding chapters on a daily basis, without having to maintain a certain level of discipline. Building your emotional intelligence isn't something you can do in a day and that's why our society is filled with scoundrels and naive people. It is essential to develop discipline to be capable and willing to dedicate yourself to developing the quality of your life.

Your emotions and discipline are interconnected. There will be moments that you'll find yourself feeling like you are losing control of your emotions and if you don't discipline yourself you could cause harm to yourself or other people.

Discipline

Discipline is often misunderstood as a concept. In particular, the majority of people see discipline as something that is akin to the notion of "walk in straight lines or you'll be punished." Discipline however, isn't the same kind of cruelty and doesn't include such punishments through corporal force. Discipline is merely the act of distinguishing right from the wrong. Discipline establishes boundaries that, if adhered to, will to make you more mature and professional. Discipline is an act of loving, rather than threats and violence.

Being disciplined is simply that you are taught to follow and adhere to the rules and codes of conduct. The goal of discipline is adhering to the institution's rules and to adhere to the code of conduct, whether you agree or not. The purpose of discipline is not to make anyone look embarrassing. The code of conduct assures everyone is acting in a manner that is respectful and is respectful to one another.

Discipline and You

Personally Discipline is the act of observing your routine, commitments promises and actions. When you've established your goals, you need to remain true to yourself by committing to these goals. If you are disciplined it will help you to recognize your own limitations and limits. If you are not disciplined then you'll be unable to accomplish any notable feat and are more likely to be abused by other people from an emotional perspective. For instance, if you're in a relationship and you maintain the discipline you have developed and discipline, your partner is more likely to treat you with respect and be more considerate of you. Additionally, being disciplined assists you in keeping your emotions under control and allows you to discern what the other person is feeling.

Building Self-Discipline

If you are looking to improve your self-control and increase your mental acuity, follow these steps:

Be determined to achieve your goals. If you've established objectives for your life, regardless of how small or large you set them, make sure to stick to these goals. The human race isn't born with discipline like they are gifted with intelligence. People become disciplined with the years and through practice. Discipline is a habit which can improve your well-being, your relationships as well as your business. Disciplined means making your priorities clear and managing your emotions, while keeping an optimistic outlook. It is essential to be committed.

Learn to prioritize your tasks. Note down an To-Do List every day in the morning or in the previous evening. List all the tasks that must be completed during the day. Start with the most important ones. You must ensure that you allotted time to accomplish what needs to be accomplished. So, all of your essential tasks will be done quickly and you'll be getting your short- and long-term objectives in no time. Another way to help you stay on track in this field is thinking about yourself as a person who has already succeeded. Begin by getting the most difficult tasks removed from your schedule before you begin working on the less stressful ones. The way you organize your priorities will help you be more efficient and you'll be looking at each day with anticipation.

Make sure you get enough sleep. There are a myriad of theories and studies about the amount of sleep that an adult needs. Some suggest an average of 8 to 9 hours rest each night, while other assert that adults require more sleep than they are able to be able to. But let's leave all of these ideas aside and recognize that in order for a successful discipline one must get enough sleep in order to remain alert and energetic the following day. Sleeping enough makes you more concentrated and able to focus on your job and priority tasks. Make a schedule for your sleep and adhere to it, making sure you fall asleep and rise at a certain time. If you are able to sleep past the time you normally sleep and you don't follow it, you're doing yourself an injustice. You'll not be able to get up on time to get up in the morning, and your focus will be diminished because of the lack of sleep. It is impossible for anything to be dealt with the next day and so, take a deep breath close your eyes and relax and get a restful and restful sleep.

Eat enough food! If your stomach isn't filled it will not let your brain work properly. It is essential to nourish your body so that it can expect it to perform for you all day long. Consume a balanced and healthy meal, that's why you should you should avoid fast food and alcohol whenever possible. The body needs healthy and "live" food items that will give us the satisfaction of making us feel happy, healthy and healthy. With all the things to do and goals eating too much will make you exhausted and unhappy. This isn't the best way to develop your mental discipline or emotional intelligence.

Find ways to keep yourself motivated. Humans are affluent. We require some sort of motivation and reward in order to complete any task. If we don't have them we often forget about our final goal and opt for an alternative route instead. To ensure that our minds are focused on our goals, whether they're long-term, or short-term, we have to devise small self-rewarding strategies to increase our motivation. Find ways to recognize your achievements since you are worthy and have earned it. Every time you feel like that you've accomplished an endeavor regardless of how small you feel, be proud of yourself as it's proof of your dedication.

Begin each day with strength and determination. Don't allow the day to pass without achieving something you are proud of. When you have developed a strong degree of discipline, you'll soon realize that your ability to manage your emotions has increased dramatically!

Chapter 5: Keys to Success to Controlling Your Emotions

If you are able to manage your emotions, you will finally take control of your life. It is essential to be aware of the reasons you make the choices you do due to the desire to alter your way of feeling. For instance, if would like to make more money, shed weight, or purchase new clothes, you're doing this due to the satisfaction you feel when you achieve your objectives. The people who are convinced that losing fat will allow them become more confident, and in turn attract more love into their lives will do whatever it takes to shed unwanted weight.

The emotions are an integral part of our lives. Instead of putting them off and burying them away they must be acknowledged them and recognize the truth in the emotions.

The Emotional Triad

Whatever situation you could be in there are three primary factors that will influence your emotions about the circumstances. Psychologists refer to these elements in the Emotional Triad which includes the three following factors:

Your Physiology

Every emotion you feel in your life is felt first by your body. If, for instance, you're looking to be more confident, you should be grounded, solid and brave when you speak. However should you wish to be more passionate within your life, then you must begin talking and moving faster. For those who wish to feel sad, just need to smile at a deep breath, sit down, and look towards the floor. The fact is that the way in which you utilize your body can result in a change in the way you feel. Motion creates emotion.

What Do You Pay Attention To?

As well as how you interact with your body, the things you pay attention to will affect the way you feel. If you'd like to be content, you must concentrate on things that bring you joy. If you can remember more happy moments from your past it will give you the foundation and opportunity to be content now. If you eliminate all positive things and experiences from your life, and instead focus on the negative and negative, you'll almost likely feel depressed. In the world of life, both good things as well as bad things are readily available. It is your choice to decide which to focus on.

Your Language

The words you choose to use can influence your mood. If you start making statements such as "I'm exhausted,"" or "I'm bored to death," the chances are that you'll be feeling tired or bored. Every word you use is accompanied by an emotional feeling to it. Certain words you choose to use can be empowering, while other are positive and encouraging. If you take care of your language, words such as metaphors, words, and phrases, you will be able to control and control your emotions.

The truth that lies behind The reality of Emotional triad is that being happy is an decision, and the same is true for depression, anger and even frustration. There's nobody who will cause you to feel happy or angry however it's based on what you make of every circumstance you come across in your daily life.

How to Handle Negative Emotions

The negative as well as positive feelings are an integral element of our lives and aren't able to be simply removed. But, you can choose to address these feelings to effectively reduce those negative ones and promote positive emotions. There are four methods in how you can handle the negative emotions.

Avoidance

Avoidance is simply a way of staying clear of situations that have the possibility of triggering negative emotions. For instance, you may avoid meeting strangers or taking chances because you are afraid of rejection or failing. It's very common for people to resort to self-medicating, such as alcohol, foodor drugs to avoid negative feelings, which is a different way of avoiding.

Denial

Denial is the act of dissociating yourself from the negative feelings that you are experiencing with statements like, "It wasn't that bad." Although you may believe it's perfectly okay to avoid acknowledging your negative feelings, this method can actually boost the negative feelings and will increase them until you begin to pay attention to those negative emotions.

Learning and using your negative Emotions

Learning to deal with how to deal with your negative emotions and making use of them is one method that can be used to handle negative emotions. The first step is to realize that all of your emotions, negative or positive are designed to help you. Your everyday emotions serve as an aid, a guidance system or a call to take action. They inform you that the task you're participating in does or doesn't.

The most important thing to be aware of is that it is you who are at the source of your feelings and that you only you can create these emotions. There is no need for a specific reason to feel a particular manner, but it's all up to you. The power to control your emotions is within you. Each emotion is a reflection of you and you are the only one competent to handle them and not just manage them but to subdue them as well. Through continued training you can make the most of your emotions, and let them work in your favor rather instead of against.

Chapter 6: Tested Techniques to Improve The Emotional Intelligence

There's no reason for you to feel discouraged if, after reading the prior chapters, you find yourself with a poor emotional intelligence. Apart from the coaching programs that you can take part in as well as other methods you can use to try for improving your EQ. Here are some strategies you can test yourself;

Learn the importance of EQ throughout all aspects of your life.

It is essential to be intelligent, but if you're emotionally smart, then more advantages are in store for you. If you have a an emotional intelligence that is high is more likely to be able to cope with any difficult circumstance and keep an enviable relationship, as well as increase your chances to work.

Be aware of anxiety triggers and take appropriate action to deal with them.

Life is full of stress-inducing situations like the sudden death of a beloved one, school, work and even failed relationships. The most important aspect of increasing the quality of one's EQ is the capacity to manage these types of stress. It is important to know what causes stress and how to relax afterward. Better still, you should be able to determine the stress triggers and eliminate them completely. In some instances it is possible to identify the cause of anxiety as well as prepare for an assault.

You should be curious about your surroundings, pleasant and easily accessible.

Being friendly and accessible is a must when discussing EQ. Always be open to new concepts because being narrow-minded is a indicator of a low EQ. If you want to think with an open mind you must be able to learn about and analyze the feelings of other people. Accept their thoughts and think about the possibilities. Keep in mind that you might not be correct. It is also important to listen to the ideas of others. By doing this it is much easier to stay calm in any stressful situation.

Be caring and welcoming.

Be aware of others as well and not just yourself. Be an extrovert. This will allow you to improve your communication skills which will result in better relationships in all aspects.

Be sure to consider all aspects with care.

Rational judgment and measurements are beneficial elements of EQ. Whatever level of understanding you have, know something If it's not implemented in a rational manner, it will be pointless. Remember that when you encounter a situation, you need to first be able to analyse the situation. Take a look at it from multiple angles and think about the implications with your rational mind, not your emotions. It's not a bad idea to analyze a situation, but do not get bogged down. After you have analyzed, stand up and take action.

Be aware and thoughtful.

Being aware means being aware of your surroundings and yourself with a positive attitude. Recognizing yourself could take some time, however the notion of being aware that you are moving towards self-improvement and awareness keeps you on an even level.

Always practice communication skills.

A person with a higher degree of communication can help you communicate and receive messages that are clear and respectful, not just within your personal boundaries but also to others.

Keep your faith in the positive.

People who always look looking up to the bright side typically lead an exciting and fulfilling life. If you're always positive about everything you do, it will be much more easy to see the beauty around you.

In a discussion with someone, don't change the subject even if are not comfortable with the topic.

Don't change your feelings quickly.

Be careful not to let go of your emotions before you have the chance to think about the situation. This way you'll be able react to it in a rational manner.

Always be sure to connect your beliefs with your emotions.

A lot of times you will experience feelings that are in conflict with the other emotions you have and that's normal. Therefore, you need to learn to differentiate between them and figure out what exactly is the cause of each. If you've accomplished this, try to connect both, and find an agreement on your beliefs and be able to better understand the issue.

Write down your thoughts and feelings.

This will be extremely helpful. Try this every once in the past, and then read your thoughts. This will allow you to gain a more objective view of your thoughts and provide you with a great perspective on your self-deprecating self. Gradually, you'll observe how your EQ is increasing significantly.

If you're not sure what you feel, ask for the opinions of other people.

It may sound strange, isn't it? It can be useful as there are instances when we are unable to comprehend our own actions. Some people may see you differently than you do. In certain situations, they are able to help you realize what's going on in your daily life better. By doing this, you'll be able to take action when it comes to the situation.

It is imperative that you understand the significance of having emotional intelligence. It can lead to positive changes for your life. If you are able to improve your emotional intelligence, it can be helpful not only in dealing with people but also with you. It will result in a better relationships in your life as well as greater understanding of your abilities. The EQ can be improved by starting with yourself. This will help you identify your strengths and how you can use them to your best benefit.

Chapter 7: The Ways of Self-improvement

Self-improvement is also desired by those who are emotionally intelligent since they are able to explore different emotions they aren't familiar with. These behaviors make them more receptive to changes and improvements.

13. They get rid of the fluttering emotions that don't contribute to self-improvement.

It's difficult for the majority of people to forget about the pain or get rid of anger they feel within themselves. A lot of people indulge in the joy and satisfaction for so long that they forget they have to deal with some issues with aggression, not in a relaxed manner. People who are emotionally intelligent are different.

They don't let their sadness and anger to be a part of them for long as they realize that letting them stay will only make them feel worse. They also pay attention to the lessons learned from the difficulties and difficulties they confront, but not the hurt. They just remember good feelings that will assist them in fighting negative emotions since they can be the sole ones that can bring advantages.

Application: Find those fleeting emotions that do not allow you to grow as an individual. They will motivate you to take a risk. Examples of such emotions include anger, sadness, jealousy anger, annoyance, and most importantly everything which makes one feel guilty. Take your fleeting feelings as books. They can be thrown away after you've read them, but what you've read will stay in your mind. The emotions are what they teach you, not what they're actually.

14. They allow their minds to dictate their emotions but do not allow their emotions to take control of their thoughts.

They let their good emotions flow freely throughout their body but do not allow their minds to be controlled. They let the negative feelings be released but do not let them control their bodies. They keep their heads over their heart, as emotions both good and bad can be controlled and managed as long as they keep their thoughts clean.

Application: Take advantage of the pride and confidence, but don't allow them to turn into boastfulness and arrogance. Take pleasure in the joy and excitement but don't let them change into apathy. Take pleasure in your happiness But don't let that hinder your development and goals. Let go of anger and frustration that are in your head, but don't let them influence your body or your actions. The good emotions you feel will help to balance the negative ones that build up inside your body, and not to deceive you.

You're always in charge of your feelings. You are the only one responsible if you allow them take over your mind and make decisions that you'll regret later on.

15. They are confident when they listen to their hearts.

Since they are confident in themselves that they are confident, they let their doubts go and focus on what they truly think. They're decisive, and they will do what is right , regardless of whether others are praising or supporting them.

Application: Don't entertain doubts when you know you're on the right track and already know what you'd like. You is deciding on your own So, seek assistance from others, but do not rely on their manipulative methods. If you're not certain of the correct answer put aside your doubts and begin searching for solutions. It's useless to think about topics you don't even know at all.

16. They are open about their feelings to others without showing any insecurity.

They are open about their feelings to those they trust with no fear because they're not afraid to display diverse emotions. They realize that both positive and negative feelings can be beneficial when utilized properly and therefore, they aren't shy about expressing how they feel. They also know that it's important to let emotions to avoid emotional rage which is harmful for the heart as well as the mind.

Application: Do not keep the emotions you are feeling even if you are aware that it could hurt someone or someone else, but also discover how and when to let out your emotions . Keeping them in will only cause you to think and behave in a way that isn't right. Make sure you have a circle of people who you can be transparent with, to relieve the pressure of your emotions. You should make a habit of a personal confession to your loved ones or an experienced counselor if you believe that you are keeping many secrets you do not even know.

17. They concentrate on the positives and forget the negative.

People who are emotionally intelligent tend to be consciously focussing on positive emotions and the things that surround them. They seek out what they can do to make more efficient use of a favorable outcome or situation but then they just forget everything else they can and let go of whatever they've already absorbed.

Useful way to practice consider the situation you're in and search for positive aspects. It doesn't matter if are caught up in the negatives since you are focused on the opposite side and not what's happening on your face. If you've not found the positive this means you're not finished on your search. When your brain is filled with positive thoughts constantly it becomes normal for you to avoid the negatives.

18. They are conscious of bringing relaxation to the body and mind.

People who are emotionally intelligent give priority to their body and mind by living a healthy life by avoiding mental and physical stress, and , most important, they can achieve the relaxation that they deserve. They strive to learn efficient ways to relax and unwind, as well as the methods that are most suitable for their particular lifestyle and their resources.

Application Relax your body and determine which relaxation methods will work for you. Are you a musician of person or who's always been the spiritual kind? Meditation or music therapy could be the right choice for you.

Are you a fan of the natural world or contemporary living? Indulging yourself in nature and owning pets are great relaxation strategies when going on an excursion to the shops and watching movies that meet your expectations of contemporary living.

Are you a person who suffers from problems with your appearance? Spa treatments and having a makeover and seeing a dermatologist most likely to help you relax most.

There is a universal concept of relaxation throughout the globe. Relaxation techniques are generally thought of as breathing exercises, meditation as well as yoga, music therapy, massage, sleeping and everything else that is that is associated with peace and tranquility. Relaxation is more of a private thing than something that's prescribed by a book. Different people have different methods to relax due to having different bodies and minds.

You're a unique set of triggers to relax joy, excitement, and peace in comparison to others. While you can find a shared thread every day however, those who haven't ever consciously created relaxation before might be unable to connect with their body and mind at first. Pay attention to your own body and mind and then take action as you like. When you are able to master this method, you will discover other techniques for relaxation which you may not however are beneficial nonetheless.

19. They are forward-thinking, but they know when to turn their gaze backwards.

They are more concerned with their emotional investment when they plan to build a stronger foundations for their emotional well-being in the near future. They are aware of how important it is to take action now to ensure a more emotionally solid future. Therefore, their mental outlook is always to serve the greater good instead of focusing on the fleeting pleasures. They think about what's more important: how they feel now or what they will be feeling later on?

But, they do look back to remind themselves of where they came from. They make use of their progress and the steps they've completed to keep themselves motivated. They stay grounded, and don't give up on their goals.

Application: Always consider the future and plan in the present. You can be the first step before other people. Be proactive and come up with solutions before problems are present. But, take time to look back when the path ahead becomes dark. Sometimes it's easier to search for direction by returning to where you began.

20. They strive for growth every time they are able to.

The most emotionally intelligent people seek out opportunities to develop not only their minds however also to improve their feelings. They're not afraid to risk their lives, whether in business or relationships since they realize the importance of going through emotional lows and highs to develop a truly resilient mindset.

Application: Don't miss out whenever an chance to experience and learn about something comes before you. The process of crossing a river that you're not used to can be uncomfortable, difficult and risky. But, remember that failing to conquer the stream will allow your strength grow and achieving in crossing the stream helps your mind explore how to navigate a new route.

21. They remain calm amidst the pressure and confusion.

They are in complete control of their emotions, even in the midst of stress and confusion. They are able to function more efficiently because they're not influenced by external influences. They let themselves serve as the leader when they see others around them losing control of their actions.

Application: Concentrate your focus on the work you have to complete and not focus on how you are feeling. Feelings is likely to fade away in the event that you do not pay attention, however the job will never complete without you keeping your cool, get your thoughts, get yourself in a good mood and do your job with calm.

22. They are preparing themselves for a continuous emotional rollercoaster.

People who are emotionally intelligent are optimistic, but anticipate the worst to be aware of potential problems that might surprise them. They are optimistic, but sensible enough to contemplate the most likely scenarios they could encounter. This helps them become more stable emotionally.

Application: Consider the most effective and least likely scenarios each day, so that you don't become frustrated when you reach low points. This will assist you in coming up with contingency plans , and help you recover with flying colours.

23. They aren't easily offended.

They remain open and seek the logic behind all that is said and done to them. They first analyze the situation before reacting and responding. Since they're blessed with confidence, they can tell what's true about them as well as what's not. They're not observant when someone tries to make them fall by relying on falsehoods.

Application: When an insulting comment or joke is made about you, take a look at the motive behind it. Do not harbor any negative sentiments towards someone who simply made a mistake , and isn't in the position of hurting you. Everybody makes mistakes at least once in a while. It's important that you tell the people close to you about the way you are feeling to not repeat the same mistake next time.

24. They release their guilt and let it go and then forgive themselves.

They're kind to themselves by letting go of guilt over the errors they did not intend to make. They make one step forward and work to improve themselves after rectifying the mess that they've accidentally started.

Application: Once you realize your mistakes and accept responsibility for them without letting pride hinder you and then accept the apology, let go of the guilt and proceed with your life. It doesn't mean you must ignore your mistakes as the lessons learned aren't over. the experiences. But, you must put aside the shame and guilt as they can create anxiety in you. You can promise yourself that you will strive to correct your mistakes and improve your character.

Chapter 8: Detachment is the key to a Great Connection

Life is a hook that draws us in. If you've attended a movie and you find yourself unconsciously absorbed in the characters and the plot Sometimes, you may even be crying. It is then clear that you have experienced a moment when you are absorbed in the narrative, and even feel as if you were in the story.

Sometimes, you can go to a movie and get so involved that even when the film ends, you need to look around in order to recall where you were. Sometimes, the drama of our lives can take over and we get caught in the narrative of our lives or even a part of our lives.

Humans all get dependent at some point throughout our life. As we grow, we are bonded to our parents as well as other caregivers. This is why attachment is seen as healthy and essential for a child's development. According to the theory of attachment unsecure attachments during childhood could cause harm to children for the rest of their life.

In the early years attachment is healthy for children however, when you are an adult, attachment is.

As adults, we can also experience patterns of attachment at work and at home. It is possible to be attached in various ways. Attachments can take many forms and shapes and. Sometimes, we are connected to people around us or to specific types of circumstances, or even substances like alcohol, for instance. Attachments that are obsessive can turn into addictions. If these types of attachments become apparent, we are likely to seek out help.

We are able to become attached to our beliefs, even if they do not satisfy us.

In our personal lives , one of the strongest bonds can be our relationship with our spouse or our opinions regarding how our lives ought to be. I was a coach for a accomplished and compassionate man whose relationship had ended apart. He was devastated. He was depressed, and for many months later, he was unable to recover his motivation or even a sense of joy. I was convinced that he would really miss his wife. I'm sure that this depressed state came due to the fact that he felt like he'd lost the beloved woman of his life? But he also admitted that the fact that he had no longer been deeply in love with the woman he was married to. He also believed they were in many ways happier without their union.

After a short time, he confessed that times ago, the man been in love with another woman. He did not pursue the love affair, however since he believed that marriage should last for the rest of time. At the time, his convictions were a blessing and helped preserve a marriage that realized had an established foundation. But his wife later was able to decide that she did not want to be part of the union which he had absolutely no influence over. This belief turned into a major issue for him. The idea that marriage could last forever was literally sucking his life. After a quick rethinking of his beliefs, he became more positive and comfortable with his circumstances.

When we work in a workplace, it is easy to frequently become entangled with one particular culture or belief in the way things are executed. We may be entangled in our views of others as well as the way relationships should be conducted at work. People who do not like changes are typically those who are enthralled by what they believe is the right way to do things.

I have been in the position of working with organizations where managers and their leaders have been enslaved to their opinions about their employees ' capabilities or their lack thereof. They also become dependent on an attitude or opinion regarding the information they're receiving.

There were times when I had a boss who was of the opinion that staff surveys were just one-time snapshots, and let employees take a stand. The manager even believed that only those who had a grudge completed the survey. The more respected employees did not have the time to fill out the survey since they were too busy performing "proper" tasks.

The manager in question was not a brand new or a narrow-minded leader in general. He was in fact an expert and a highly competent high-level manager. Despite efforts to provide him with another perspective He preferred to believe in his own view and his views prevailed. The results of his survey did not get better.

Letting go of attachments can provide us the freedom to live the life we want to

Childhood attachments can provide assurance in an unpredictable world. As we grow older, attachments may cause us pain and suffering as we must often and with great resistance, let go of attachments. We may have to admit that we might have been not thinking or believing the right things. It is possible to increase the doubt we're trying avoid.

Attachment to anyone in any form is harmful, regardless of whether it's a belief of a person or an habit. Most of the time, we don't realize we're affixed to someone or something until we face physical or emotional changes. Attachment is actually a response to anxiety. It's also a part of human nature so there's nothing to be down about!

What is the solution? Everyone needs to establish connections with each other and to situations. We must create an understanding of our thoughts and beliefs so that we can be successful. Here are some methods to help us manage our lives.

There are a variety of ways to transform attachments into more healthy relationships.

As we mature, we are able to recognize the signs that we are connected to certain people, and then change the focus to healthy relationships. The concept of connection is healthy method of connecting without the anxiety basis that attachment entails. We can connect in a deep way to our most intimate relationships. If you can connect with other people, you feel more free and more than one another.

If we have a strong attachment to certain objects or habits like your car, or purchasing new clothes every month or even your house or your house, then getting rid of these attachments could cause stress or even unhappiness.

In those circumstances, attachments just become painful as a result of, for instance that we might be purchasing new clothes every month and losing our job. If our spouse gets an offer to work and we are required to relocate to Australia and that would mean having to leave the home that we've been living in.

If we have to let go of attachments, we must rethink the relationship we have with them. We should explore alternative options and open ourselves to a different perspective, however there is a lot of resistance that can be very stressful. If we are able to achieve an attitude that is different from ours, where we were able to appreciate these things but not relying on them: We remain open to new possibilities and stay clear of unnecessary discomfort.

We have to be free of our desire to conform. Beliefs, attitudes, and concepts, as well as emotional reactions could limit our lives in a huge way. The way we live our lives is determined by our convictions. What we believe in shapes our reality. Through keeping an open mind and being ready to look at our reactions patterns as well as our beliefs and thoughts by being ready to change them as needed; we remain open and fresh to whatever life throws our way.

Finally, we can be consciously positive. It is important to recognize the signs that we're being negative and the ways in which this could limit us and others within our homes and workplaces. Remaining in negative opinions and conclusions could prove us wrong at the end of the day.

If we could be able to recognize the times we're attached and then, with compassion towards ourselves, let go of the attachments we have and substitute them with more loving and conscious alternatives, our lives will be happier and more enjoyable.

Chapter 9: The Reasons Why Gaining Emotional Intelligence is Essential

Have you ever felt an emotion that you didn't know about and could not describe the emotion during a tense moment? Perhaps you've encountered an awkward situation in which you were unable to figure out why your lover seemed so upset Perhaps you were a boss, or a coworker who stayed away from your concerns due to a reason which was unnoticed by you. The ability to comprehend yourself and others in a way that is emotional, can be beneficial in all aspects in your daily life. It can even bring advantages for your pets, if you've the ability to comprehend how they feel.

If you're reading this book probably haven't experienced the advantages of having an emotional intelligence since you've never been through it. Therefore, in order to provide you with an opportunity to boost your emotional intelligence, let's take a an overview of the ways it can impact your life.

Personal Benefits

Then, we'll discuss the obvious advantages that emotional intelligence can bring to your own life. In relation to you, the ability to express emotions will improve your mental health by relieving anxiety and helping you to avoid unpredictable mood fluctuations. If this occurs the physical health of your body will be improved. You can manage your own health by controlling your stress levels which have a significant effect on the overall health of your body. Only by taking control to manage your emotions can you reduce stress and anxiety in your life.

But, there are few benefits that are not widely known about having a high level of emotional intelligence. People with emotional intelligence have more optimism and are always working towards a goal whatever it is, be it an individual or professional goal. A person who is emotionally intelligent is a person who has a mindset of growth and can overcome any obstacle. This helps them be more successful both at home and at work.

People with these traits are often motivated by their own inner desire more than motivated by an external goal. The people with higher level of emotional intelligence perform better because they know they have accomplished a task with success. So, no matter the goal you set to accomplish in your life, you'll be content when you achieve the end goal, whether that is simply knowing that you have achieved the objective or earning an amount of money. This will make you more inclined to set goals that can bring you money.

Alongside being more optimistic and being able to feel proud when you achieve goals rather than filling your pockets You'll also be more kind towards others and yourself. One of the most significant advantages of having emotional intelligence is the ability to return the favor to yourself with compassion. It allows you to recognize when you're being too busy and you need a break. when you're being overly critical of yourself for a mistake and to recognize when you tried the best you could.

A big part of being compassionate and goal-oriented is controlling your own thoughts and feelings, as well as being aware of your self. People who are emotionally intelligent can handle any difficult situation, whether it's a work or personal one. They know how to remain in control and manage their emotions so that they don't cause embarrassment for their own or other people. If you're more aware of yourself it's possible to recognize the strengths as well as weaknesses to make use of them and enhance your skills.

Benefits of Relationships

One of the benefits of being emotionally aware is being aware of the state of mind of your companion in relationships, whether it's one of friendship, romance or familial relationship. Being aware of someone else's emotional state will help you manage your responses and is the sole factor you're in control of in any dispute or conversation. Let's examine the benefits specific to every kind of relationship.

Benefits of a Romantic Relationship

Are you puzzled by the sudden silence of your partner in the course of a relationship? Perhaps you've been in the situation that you could not keep your temper until you exploded and then said something more inflamatory? All of us have.

However, emotionally intelligent people can figure out the reasons for their partner's lack of communication. Could it be because someone close to them has passed away and now they're trying to deal with their grief by clenching up? Perhaps they're extremely upset over the fact that you didn't do the dishes in the evening, and feel you're not upholding to the terms of your deal. Whatever the case the issue, being emotionally wise can assist you in resolving the problem before it becomes a crisis.

The fact that you have an emotional brain helps you help your friend, but can also help you to assist yourself when you are in a heated argument. You'll be able to detect the warning signs of going towards and outbursts and swiftly steer yourself away from any unhelpful actions during a disagreement.

Friendship or Familial Relationships

The lack of communication between family members or even friends is not uncommon, and most times people are disappointed when they let these situations to go on for the length of time they can. Being able communicate your issues and take note of the concerns of others helps you sympathize with the other person of the conflict and helps to resolve the issue faster. Wouldn't it be nice in the event that you were able to get over an unpleasant incident instead of focusing on it for long?

Business Relations

There are a variety of ways that being emotionally smarter can benefit you in your career. For example, if must work in an team knowing how to read the body language of your team members will allow you to manage anger before it becomes outright anger. Also, being capable of controlling your emotions during heated debates can demonstrate to your coworkers and the team leader that you're able to function when faced with a difficult circumstance, which could lead to promotions in pay, higher wages, and greater job satisfaction.

Outside of the company You'll be able deal with customers and clients better if you can discern how they're feeling and reacting to body language and messages you're trying to convey. Particularly working in sales emotional intelligence can aid you in recognizing when you're trying to impress a client and/or client or if you're in the process of securing the deal.

Workplace Benefits

The ability to be emotionally intelligent can be a huge help when it comes to work bringing advantages such as improved teamwork and a more conducive office and more flexible adjustments, improved time-managementand management capabilities.

Team-Work

If members of the team even one are more emotionally intelligent they are more adept at completing their duties. People with more emotional intelligence communicate with their colleagues better than those who aren't attuned to the emotions of others. A person with more emotional intelligence can communicate their thoughts to othersand is more open to other's thoughts. The less they are likely the initiative in a situation without thinking about their coworkers first. A person with higher emotional ability is more likely to respect their colleagues and appreciate their contributions.

Office Environment

People who are emotionally intelligent are naturally an increase in morale for the workplace. If you work with an office filled with people who are able to get along and respect one another and can resolve conflicts peacefully work environments improve by default. It's a much better workplace. If you'd like to work in a setting that encourages innovative ideas and goals, as well as supportive and generally, an ideal place to work to be, then you must become emotionally competent and help others achieve the same.

Easier Adjustments

It is essential for businesses not to stagnate and their employees. Through continuous self-improvement and self-improvement, you'll be able to keep up with the pace of your company and become more effective as an employee. This will lead to advantages for you in the near future.

While you might not accept changes within the business with open arms but you'll be able to see that these changes are made for the benefit of the entire company and have nothing to directly impact your own performance. Removing yourself from the current situation and acknowledge that you are not responsible for the changes taking place.

Better Time-Management

People with higher emotional intelligence are aware of when it's time to get their feet on the ground and complete the task as opposed to an employee who is slack because they're not "feeling it' on the day. One of the biggest benefits of having a strong emotional intelligence while working is the ability to put aside any problems outside of the workplace you may be facing and focus on the job to be completed. This can help you be more productive within the workplace and can lead to great rewards in the long run: better pay and time off as well as better benefits and greater respect from your bosses even if you have issues that can't be overlooked.

Leadership Capabilities

If you're emotionally smart, you'll can become an effective leader, as well as being a better leader when you're already in an executive position. It's about being able to manage your emotions and also being able to discern the feelings of other people. One of the ways that to benefit from this in your leadership role is to be able to tell the signs that a member of your team isn't comfortable with the role they're in. It is easy to determine the specifics of their job that are making them uncomfortable or even move their job if the one they're currently in doesn't work out. The first step to doing this is to recognize that the team member isn't acting with confidence.

All of us can improve the level of our emotions, not just those who already have these traits. The chaos that exists in our world will never improve if we don't be a bit more emotionally smart. Therefore, you can make the world better by following the steps and recommendations found in this guide.

Chapter 10: Programming Yourself To Be successful

Being able to control your emotions means knowing that you can do anything if you choose to act. If you focus on positive emotions and thoughts You can also take the steps towards confidence in yourself. You can improve your observance and curious, compassionate and perhaps even effective.

This is the perfect moment to let go of any previous beliefs you held regarding success. This chapter will guide you to transform your thinking about success. You can learn all about how to program your mind to think and attract about success.

It's funny to see how people believe that hard work will bring success, but when they get started they get little to none of the outcomes. What is the reason for this? If all your focus is to work harder than yesterday, it's true that you'll put in more effort then you were the previous day ...

however, this is it. If you're focused on the end result, feeling relaxed, on feeling happy, relaxed, on the idea of yourself reaching this objective and being happy with the results it will differ.

Focus is an amazing instrument and, if we employ it in the right manner it can accomplish so more than we ever capable of. The focus on working hard and focusing on your goals are two distinct things. You can organize the steps you'll need to take to succeed however focusing on these steps is different than focusing on your success in itself.

How can you prepare yourself to achieve success?

The first thing to be aware of is the reality that you're in contest with others; rather, you're in contest with yourself. If you're looking to get more efficient, you must be more successful than you were yesterday or the month before or the previous year. Set this as your goal to push you forward. This means you will be able to observe the improvements you've made each month, or the year in and year out. The sensation you'll feel as you view your personal and professional growth over time is unimaginable. It will feel like (and it's true) you've entered an entirely different world because we're not the same person as we were one year ago. If you've been characterized by not acknowledging your achievements and comparing your achievements or the progress you've made in your life to your colleagues or friends, siblings or even your spouse, it's time to let go of these thinking patterns. They're not helping you in any way. All they'll do for you is to put you in a negative mood, reduce your energy and put you in a bad place. Don't let yourself be the reason why that you aren't successful.

If you're doubtful of positive thoughts and their benefits It's moment to begin practicing it. In the text, you've read many chapters on the benefits that is positive thought. You might be the biggest doubter on the planet If you decide to try this technique you'll be amazed by how simple it is.

For each negative thoughts you've got you have, try to think of three positive ideas. You can beat your thoughts of "I cannot do this" by thinking "I could", "I will" or "Nothing can stop me from doing what I want to do". You're the one in the complete control of your thoughts. You're the one to say "enough will suffice". Start your day by chanting affirmations (you are able to make up yourself). Instead of thinking that it will be another tough day with no results or poor collaborations with coworkers, keep your eyes on the goal you have set. See yourself reaching your objective. See yourself being successful. Think about how this will be achieved and then let yourself get to the depths of the details as you'd like. Make yourself smile at the mirror, and breathe deeply. This is yours. You're alive and well-nourished, you have an occupation and a target and there's no way that anything could hinder you from achieving your goals.

People who regularly practice affirmations and train their minds to be positive typically say that they have seen rapid changes in their lives. These changes could take the form of uncluttered streets on the way to work, finding cash on the streets, or receiving unintentionally a message with a great job or collaboration offer or collaboration, etc.

Do not be afraid of meditation. Many people believe that they're not suited to practice meditation because they're emotional, stressed , or unhappy to remain still for long periods of time. Everyone can practice meditation without having to spend money on an instructor or for assistance from a meditation consultant to help you. On the internet, you can find numerous free guided meditations to help you with everything you require (success in relaxation, relaxation, sleeping getting love, being more mindful, and so on).

Meditation can have a remarkable effect on the human mind as well as body. It can help you unwind and clear your mind and be aware of what's happening within you. It will teach you how to relax and breathe deeply, and be able to see the benefits for your whole body. Additionally, a daily practice for 15 minutes to an hour is suggested by psychologists and physicians. It's an excellent way (along with exercise) to lower anxiety and to become more conscious of yourself and your thoughts. A brief practice can improve your perception as your intuition is reactivated and you'll be able to pinpoint exactly what you're looking for, you'll be able visualize things with greater ease and you'll be able to rest better. Certain meditations have affirmative phrases which means you'll reap the benefits of two from it.

Make sure you take action to move in the direction you've established your goals. For instance, if an author who wants to create the next great novel, you should begin to research the subject matter you'd like to write about. Write down your thoughts and ideas, imagine your characters, then open the Word document and begin writing.

Don't forget to be happy. It appears that recently, people have forgotten to be happy. It's not necessary to wait around for something big to occur. You'll feel better when you are seeing the sunshine of the day. Feeling good is since you're healthy and you have friends, or because you're heading out on an extended vacation within two weeks. Find the little things you can be happy about. Be happy, sing in the loudest possible way when your favourite song is playing on the radio, smile or do activities that make you feel happy, and be with people that make you feel great. These small things are essential for your health and well-being ... also, don't let them go unnoticed. It's not difficult to feel angry and frustrated with the world around you, and to think of yourself as someone that can't do anything. You can blame the world for your troubles, or take the responsibility for your actions and make use of every resource you have and invest in yourself for the future. It's your the choice you make.

In order to program your brain to be successful you could even record your goals. Be sure to write it all with the present time for example "I am an author published" and "I am making 30 percent more than I earned in the past". The present is a way of expressing that the situation is taking place right now. Do not let your mind convince you otherwise in the hope of rationalizing that you're not a published writer (yet) or your pay is the same (for the moment). It's even possible to note these goals/affirmations down on a notepad and stick them in visible locations like the fridge or in the vanity mirror of your bathroom. Let these affirmations and goals linger on your mind and observe how quickly they occur.

Another way to train yourself to succeed is to design an image board. There are plenty of images of things you would like to attain or already are currently (pictures of a lovely workplace, your ideal home and money, clothing you'd like to put on and so on) and then pin them to the vision board. If you're not keen to cut out images from magazines then you can go about this more easily - create an image as a wallpaper for your smartphone or computer with the things you'd like to accomplish. Set it up for your eyes to constantly see it and allow it to get in your mind.

Feel good about your goal. Feel the feelings you'll experience when you meet your desired goal. Feel free to be happy, smile or feel joyous (this occurs when you do a lot of detailed visualizations of your goals). It can alter your energy level and emotional state, and instantly bring you into a better mood.

Chapter 11: The Slave Of The Machine

Welcome to the twenty-first century! Welcoming to the next century. Here are your zillion social network accounts. This is your home email address as well as your shopping email and your email for work, and a myriad of other online accounts. This is your phone and a hundred contacts who will send you texts daily or once a year. Here's the latest news on your top films, sports teams or bands. You can stream live TV all over the world and here's a zillion distracting things that the grandparents weren't forced to fight and wrestle with to keep their attention. Welcome to the mind meat grinder.

We are dependent on technology. It's simple and straightforward and technology can be a wonderful master or lover. No question about it. However, it's murder on your body, flesh and blood connections. If you're in need of proof and don't want to see yourself in the mirror go to your nearest coffee shop or restaurant. After you've had a seat and become comfortable, glance around. You'll see how many people are using laptops or using their phones, conversing via their mobiles, or gaming on the phones. It's not something that's healthy, especially when you're around other people. In reality, you'll be surrounded by peopleall connected to their phones.

Phones are fantastic devices and tools to help you live your life more easily however they shouldn't be the sole focus of your life. If you are unable to have conversations without taking your phone on or capable of being in the moment, then you've got an issue. Don't get scared or feel that you're the only one in this, as there are thousands of people who have the same issue as you and that's because the majority of us are connected to the internet. There's definitely something wrong however, what does it mean? What can you do to fix this in order to be free?

As with everything there is always a beginning with the baby steps. The first step is to realize that there are essential sources that we can use with our phones, and there are the frivolous ones that we utilize. Be aware of the distinction. When someone is trying to contact you from workplace, it's crucial. Also, a or text message from loved ones, family members or friends who require you at the moment. All else is unnecessary and also recreational. Take a minute to consider what is essential and what's not in regards to your phone.

If you are aware of the priorities you have and what you want to achieve, it's easy to figure out where you could reduce your expenses. Be aware that you don't have enough time to check out sports scores news, news stories news, updates from bands movies trailers, and so on. Consider all the time you'll have on your own to review that information and arrange your schedule in a way that is appropriate. So when you are seated with your friends, it's simple to move on to another step.

This is the time to pay attention to the person you're sharing it with. Do not waste your time with one person because they're in the moment with you because of a reason. It could be that they are in love with you, they love you or they need to be with you and want to share something together, and not take the time to check your Facebook. Unplugging from your phone is among the most beneficial ways to improve your personal life and for your relationships.

In the previous chapter, we talked about how crucial it is to pay attention to the people whom you're with, and that you should spend the mental energy fully understanding the conversation in order to make the most of it. Take away any distractions that hinder your ability to be present with those who are around you. You'll notice the difference immediately and the others around you will as well. This is just good manners and it'll really bother you when you realize that other people don't show the same respect.

Don't become dependent on the machines that are in your life. The Internet brings the world closer closer every day and with the cost of the people right in your path. Be respectful and begin to disconnect. The difference will be evident instantly in the relationships between your and with those closest to you. People will feel more appreciated when you are sitting next to them and switch your phone off or at the very least, on vibrate. Baby steps, remember. Baby steps.

Chapter 12: Maintain Your Principles

Interacting with other people does not need you to abandon your beliefs. When you speak with others, be honest and genuine. Be true to what you say and never lie for intention of making the other person feel better.

As was explained in the previous lesson, when you are interacting to another person, you simply attempt to get to know them or them. You put yourself in their shoes and comprehend why they hold certain opinions, or beliefs or what they are feeling. It does not necessarily mean that you agree or disagree with their opinion or opinion on a particular subject.

This is a trap that many people do not realize they are in. Since they are constantly listening and observe the people whom they meet, emotionally intelligent people can spot the inconsistencies of other people's words.

This can lead one to two conclusions: that the person isn't reliable, or, even more importantly, manipulative or is a weak person who is easily manipulable.

Whatever conclusion they come to the idea of keeping a distance from the other person is the best option and means that it is impossible to establish any type of social connection.

The necessity to keep your beliefs only adds to the need to practice meditation or, at minimum self-awareness.

Exercise 6

A majority of people do not know what their position is on a particular issue until they are confronted with an opposing opinion. It is the default mentality of the majority of humans to believe that if one believes in something as real, the rest the world accepts the same thing as true. When confronted with another statement people are either engulfed in disbelief followed by confusion and eventually anger, or avoid conflicts, even though they believe that they are not, they accept and agree with the assertion.

So, in the lesson 6 exercise prior to the time that unthinkable, negative ideas can catch you off guard it is important to know your self. This is an exercise in which meditation will play a key part. There is no better way to know yourself apart from contemplation and reflection.

There isn't any method or system to meditate since it's an inner process that is not a way to know the inner workings of your mind, nor can anyone be in control of it. Here are some general tips to help you get through meditation:

As previously mentioned to separate your thoughts from your own, pick a subject to focus on and then observe the subject from a distance. The object could be anything, including an

Instead of thinking about the facts that you already know, think about questions about what you're not yet aware of or would like to learn. For instance, terrorism can be something that the world is aware of as being harmful and there is no doubt about it. But , it is possible to ask whether there's someone who is convinced of the contrary. Additionally, consider what terrorists' own thoughts about their actions.

In simple meditation, obtaining an answer isn't required. It's just important that you accept the notion that what you believe isn't absolutely true.

Then, consider your reasons for why, in spite of an opposing viewpoint it is your decision to adhere to what you believe in. It is preferable to support your beliefs with previous memories and facts.

It may seem like you're thinking too much however, it's really not the case. Be aware that when you meditate you're being conscious. It is not a matter of rushing between thoughts to let the thoughts that are associated with the thought affect your. This is an extension of the practice of self-awareness.

Chapter 13: Staying Informed and Interessed

Individuals who consider themselves emotionally smart are more up current than other people. They are involved in the world that surrounds them and actively participate in the community in which they reside. They don't consider themselves being isolated from their surroundings and are content to be updated. Check out the following questions and see what you can answer. If you are unable to solve them in a precise manner then it's the right time to begin reading and learn more about the world that you reside in:

* How many people reside in the area where you reside?

* What's the name given to the mayor of the town in which you reside?

* Why do people cut down on the use of plastic?

Are you doing something to benefit the surroundings?

Are you aware of the best ways to lessen the carbon footprint of your home?

Do you know why you got sick the last time you suffered?

If you're not able to find the answers to these questions, you might not be as smart emotionally as you think. While these might appear to be something that can be measured solely by intelligence but your emotional involvement in your life is just essential. When you aren't feeling a strong desire for something, you'll never know how to bring that passion to the forefront and get the most out of your existence. So, the issues raised above can be relevant to the world around you and are things you might want to be looking into more.

To be an emotional savvy person You must open yourself open to the new. If you don't enjoy something is it because of something, do you know the reason? Write down a list of things you do not like and then discuss the reasons. What do you think about how you feel in a natural space? Are you more at ease? Do you feel more relaxed? Are you at peace? What does this mean is the ability to turn off whenever you want to, and simply take in the world around you are, without letting thoughts of another aspect of your day interrupt the pleasure.

You might have noticed that those around you are engaged in activities or meditation. They may also be participating with yoga sessions or anything like that. The reason they participate in these classes - apart from the obvious necessity to stay fit is because they want to be focused, and taking part in these classes helps them to become.

To determine the extent to which you must concentrate on something that allows your mind let go of negative thoughts Try this. If you ever find yourself feeling extremely negative at all times, find the natural surroundings and take a deep breath and focus on your breathing and try not to think about what your negative thought is. Do you have the ability to do this? People who are emotionally intelligent are able to shut off their emotions that keep them back. They might use their free time activities to to resist these negative thoughts.

If you've never attempted to meditate, do this. Relax on a firm chair and hold your spine straight. Inhale into your nostrils until 7 seconds and then exhale at the rate of 8. Concentrate on breathing and take a moment to release any thoughts. I'd like to bet you're not able to do it. The thoughts of our mind are everywhere of the day, however there are way too many thoughts for a typical man to manage.

What you must do is get rid of the thoughts that have no value in your life, except to distract you from your goals. Imagine your thought is like a balloon. Close your eyes for one second and imagine the thought as balloons. It is possible to continue to observe it and be negative or just allow it to go. Imagine the balloon flying away and then let go of the thought without making any judgements about the thought at all. You can even blow up the balloon into your brain's eye and let go of your negative thoughts that race through your head. If you do enough exercise for something and it becomes an habit. This is how habits form.

They are actions you repeat over and over again that your subconscious brain learns upon your actions. If you think that a thought of a specific nature causes your blood pressure increase regularly it is likely that you've developed a pattern that's not very emotionally smart. But, if you just blow up the balloon or let it disappear without judging every time you think about it then you will begin to build an underlying habit that allows you to be more emotionally well-informed and not be affected due to your emotional state. You're dealing with your struggles without letting them take over you.

Explore an interest that will give you plenty of knowledge. Be sure to stay informed about current events and if are looking for answers to questions regarding things in your life, explore these. The more comprehensive the scope that you know, the more easy it will be to apply the knowledge to the relationships you are in, making you aware of other people and the pain they, too, suffer.

We often view things from a single perspective If you're open to learning, you are also aware of things that you might not have thought of. This helps you think about things from different perspectives that are different from your personal. This is a sign of emotional intelligence since when people approach you with questions it is not enough to think that you know the answer and will do your best to offer them the best solution you can. Learning to be open allows you to become multi-dimensional in your thinking and that's the essence of life an experience of learning that never ends from the moment of birth until death.

Chapter 14: What to Change Your Mind to not be angry

The unconscious and conscious mind are constantly communicating with one another. There is a boundary that we all cross daily. It is a border that we cross often without being aware of the consequences. In the evening, as we sleep at night, and in the early first morning when we rise up. We cross a threshold one that divides two worlds. Who tells you it's time to sleep when you're not conscious? If the reality is just the interpretation that your brain creates from the electrical signals it receives from its five senses when we go to sleep what happens?

The world that surrounds you is nothing more than the exact reconstruction of the vibrations of the soul. An emotional state, or the vibrational offer, alters the matrix and sends signals to demand a certain life-style: Anima asks, God will answer. This idea has changed the lives of many particularly after finding proof as well as evidence from the field of science.

The world you live in can be described as the result of thoughts and emotions. What you consider to be real is just an illusion. Okay, here we are. When we are able to understand this, what are we left to do? We all agree that everything is illusion However, how can create an illusion the I would like it?

The power of the vibrational offering of gratitude can bring happiness, this is an unpopular but proven fact instantly. If you feel grateful, it instantly propels you into your most positive emotional state. worry melts away, tensions disappear, and joy comes in and goes to fill the void that was caused. Being grateful connects us with the whole in that it makes us worthy of the things we require.

If you change the way that you perceive things,

The things that can be changed

Being grateful lets us immediately connect to the subconscious brain, that is sensitive to everything that creates emotion in us. The emotion of gratitude is among the most intense emotions can be experienced simply by focusing our attention on the present moment and everything that life has so far provided us.

The subconscious mind is the one that guides your life and everything you believe you're doing is being recommended to you by that portion of your brain that doesn't appear to be there, the section of yourself that is able to hear every sound and responds to anything.

The automatic emotional reactions that are often triggered in specific situations are that is stored on an unconscious level. If the mind's unconscious realizes that it is in the situation it has already experienced, it gives you the rational or emotional response that it previously thought best suited for the present.

Let me clarify what I mean: do you know how your browser functions in order to connect to the internet? When you browse the internet, the browser saves preferences and data so that when you come back to browse it will be simpler for him to offer you the best possible solutions to the kind of research you normally conduct. The unconscious mind functions the same way. You can register and suggest the best solutions for you. take all the necessary steps to protect yourself and ensure the most pleasant experience. However, often the information you receive is inaccurate outdated, harmful, and not relevant to the times we live. What do you think? perhaps it's time to upgrade the system periodically or not? Or the psychoquantistic approach maybe it's time to modify the model and change the mind ! ?

If you were twenty years ago and humiliated yourself before the girl you loved, it is not logical to repeat that embarrassing experience. However, the unconscious of not receiving any additional details of the incident in the course of time in that situation, is likely to offer you the same logical or emotional product should you encounter her again. The trick is to suggest new thoughts and feelings regarding the event in the event that you happen to come across it.

In the end, and referring back to the point made in the beginning, there are two points at which we pass through the two realities that reside with our lives: the moment we first wake up and sleep. Between these two points, our experience of life and perception of reality change. We leave one world to go to another. The two worlds have been fighting one another since we were born. And since the moment we were born, we can nothing but go in and out. Did you believe you've only had only one life? Instead, you have two.

If in the day, our rational mind allows us to be immersed in the physical reality that is presented to us, in the night, in the deep sleep stage, it's the unconscious mind who takes the reigns of our dreams life. The rational mind remains in a state of silence and is able to observe the beauty the unconscious mind has to present. It is exactly the same whenever we meditate, or give us to live free of any logical or rational intrusions which is when we look at without judgment , the world around us or allow ourselves to be in a state of flow through what we see.

It is just the few seconds before reaching the threshold of two worlds that magic could be created. Miracles are literally planted in this area. Have you ever sunk to sleep thinking of a problem you needed to work out and the next day, you had the solution in your mind as if it came from nowhere like a bolt out of the blue? Every request is is always fulfilled and accepted. It's possible to refer to it as God the unconscious or Soul the power to the brain, name whatever you want however this characteristic separates you from other SOUL-li on the world. Your mind is in the process of creating yourself all the time and those five minutes prior to the time you go to bed are crucial to shape the world you wish to experience.

THE FINAL 5 MINUTES OF the day

THEY ARE THE BEGINNING OF YOUR NEW WORLD

Be aware of the last moments before you go to bed can enhance your quality of life. The day is nearing close and the rational mind is urging your subconscious to take total control of your abilities. At this point of transition, we can suggest to the subconscious mind what it needs to focus on, and in what area of our lives requires assistance.

Many people, in complete ignorance of their power, will spend the final five minutes of their day composing an account of their past hours. They also highlight the negative elements of what happened during the day. They think about the potential offenses they may have endured, and trigger resentment. revisit fears and anxieties about what could have been and will occur.

They're telling their subconscious to manage every worry, without using the opportunity to work towards the things they want to be able to see manifest throughout their life. It's like having the castle that has a hundred rooms and being a stable. It's like having a million dollars and then continuing to purchase things that aren't needed. What can we do to ensure that inside us is the ability to accomplish what we want , if we don't ever think about it?

The subconscious of our mind must come in contact with what we desire rather than the things we don't wish for. If you continue to think about what you don't wish for (before you fall asleep) You'll be experiencing what you don't desire. It's like the equivalent of a snake biting its tail. If you want to reverse this mental model and be aware of the things you'd like to achieve in your life. Be a part of the tomorrow's self who created it. What will you do? Who will you have with you? Who will be elated of your accomplishments?

Take advantage of the benefits realizing your dreams will bring. In the mind of the unconscious, it doesn't matter whether it is real or isn't. He will offer you the best way to finish your task of him, as if he was your employee. You can tell him what you want him to accomplish and he with utmost accuracy, will accomplish it.

Paying attention to our dreams and desires prior to bed, allows the unconscious to process it. Have you heard the word G.I.G.O? It is utilized for computer sciences and refers to garbage inside garbage out. This means that when you program your computer to work with garbage information garbage information is all you receive.

The result of your subconscious mind will be of the same character as the food you put in it. Work on the worries and fears you'll receive. Focus on your dreams and you'll find by magic, the right tools and the appropriate strategies to manifest them.

Decide to be THE SOLUTION, not the issue

The world of life is filled with endless possibilities. There are no limit, we must choose. Utilize your imagination to create what you desire and not things you don't want. In the last five minutes of your day, you will be transformed emotionally into the person who succeeded to accomplish his goal, not stuck in the current situation.

You might have to instruct yourself to do this, particularly when you've never tried this before. It is likely that you will have to alter your lifestyle and you'll have remove your smartphone and turn off your TV and commit yourself to dreaming about the life you'd like to live. This can be your only chance to get to your goal.

When you pay attention to, you will feel the energy flow there. If you focus your attention prior to sleeping the reality you choose to manifest will begin there. Don't be afraid of your future make it!

If you keep on following the same pattern of behavior the same way, you'll never alter your life. If there's something you are not happy about you dislike, make it a priority to alter it. Most people complain about every aspect, but they don't take the initiative to implement a drastic change within their own lives. Remember this mantra: "if you really want to achieve a better outcome it is necessary to act differently".

It may seem logical and straightforward when spoken of, however in reality it's not always. Human creatures are habitual. We prefer to repeat things to ease our lives, or in fear of being in the dark or to not need to think about alternatives. But, we're always prepared to be criticized or to complain. It would not be more convenient to be productive and make one's path to success? One could argue that this is already written, but it's equally true that in the near future, one "must be aided a bit".

It takes time several experiences, and numerous occasions in order to "program" the brain. The way we think is determined by our personalities as well as the way we interact with people, by the level of education we have received and received, from achievements at work, etc. The good thing is that the mind is able to "reprogram" the same way as using a computer or mobile phone. This "reset" can be used to confront our present, and more importantly, all to look into the future in a more effective way , by removing everything that is not beneficial and doesn't allow us to advance.

If you're looking to make changes the way you think about it, the first thing you should do is ask yourself what you are looking to accomplish by doing it. It's not required for others to be able to answer the question. Try this exercise when you're in your home, at work while in the pool, or when you travel.

The other most important question to ask yourself is "Why should I take this action?". Perhaps you're unhappy because you're looking for the perfect love, but it doesn't appear, or because you are trying to get a degree or need to be promoted. There is probably no reason not to continue the desire to become better than a "better individual".

Explore ways you can alter your behaviour and how long it will take to accomplish it. Be honest and objective Your date must not be extremely distant nor close in time.

The mind's programming begins from the moment we are born, the very first moment in our lives. It is influenced by the instruction of our parents as well as the lessons by our educators. While personality is a source of influence but relationships are far more crucial. If you are looking to program the same way as the PC, you need to create a new program that meets your requirements and demands.

It has been proven by neuroscientific studies that humans communicate with themselves around 14 hours per day. In that conversation, 90 percent of the messages are negative. "I don't understand everything", "I can not accomplish this", "it's very difficult", "I'm too clumsy", "I always arrive late", "this is not for me" are just a few of the most frequently used phrases that pop into your the mind . For the computer analogy they are similar to viruses that damage your system. All you need to do is install an antivirus that is reliable and remove the malware that has accumulated on an extremely crucial parts of your body: the mind.

The memories of the past form your present and determine your future. If you don't behave as a leader today then you'll not be the next day. If you believe that you will not get the one you've always wanted to be with today, you may not be able to meet it until tomorrow. We must change the way we think to meet our objectives.

When you are aware that your conversations begin to become negative and you begin to feel depressed, repeat affirmations that are positive. By doing this, you'll eliminate them, just as do the clouds in the sky, when it's very windy.

Three steps to program the brain

1-Repetition: train your mind to repeat an affirmation repeatedly as often that you are able to. This will increase neural activity and will remove, as mentioned previously, negative ideas. Rethink the negative thoughts that are damaging your brain.

2. Reminder: Your mind can cause you to forget the things you'd like to change because of the "resistance in a change". Imagine that in your brain, there's someone who manages the program, but they're reticent about changing their routines. You have to be a disciplined and

strict leader so that your employee will follow the demands of your boss. The issue is that you are unable to remove him from the job, which means you must manage your employees to follow the rules.

3Visualization: Every day for 5-10 minutes, you are required to consider your goals. Imagine being in that exact situation and feeling the emotions that come up. Add additional details to the portrait until the scene appears completed.

The most common reaction to uncertainty is anxiety, worry and fear. The future, that wonderful stranger, tends to create similar feelings. However, the future isn't entirely black, and we can change it to make it better. The future is too uncertain to predict however, we can take some mindsets that can enable us to deal with the future with a positive outlook.

There are many options to deal with the future. Because it is yet to happen and we don't know which events will occur.

Making predictions about the future is a futile method, and it could lead to negative mood swings.

Four of them stands out, which, generally they represent in a straightforward and visual manner the complete spectrum of mental attitudes can be assumed:

Ostrich's attitude (passivity)

The attitude to the man who is a fireman (reactivity)

The attitude of the insurance company (prevention)

The attitude that the conspirator has (proactivity).

The ostrich and the passive

The ostriches, in contrast to what people believe they do not bury their head beneath the ground when they sense risk. However, the behavior of the ostrich is founded exactly on this notion and that is, they do absolutely nothing to face the dangers. This inaction hinders us from being aware of what the reality of the universe is, until the shifts force them, sometimes in all their savagery.

The ostrich as well as the passivity

Ostriches, contrary to what people believe that they don't hide their head when they see risk. However, the behavior of the ostrich rests exactly on this notion and that is to do nothing when faced with dangers. The ostrich's passive attitude keeps us from being aware of what the reality of the universe is until the change imposes them, sometimes with all their force.

This kind of attitude is considered negative because it implies having no idea the eventuality that can happen to us. But, this isn't always. In reality, liability is an effective strategy, and at times even efficient but it is not without risk. If we mimic the ostriches, we may lose significant opportunities.

Reactivity and Firefighter

Firefighters typically act once the fire has begun and is no longer prevented. This approach to the future is more active than the Ostrich, and involves watching for fires to grow until they can eliminate it. In the meantime, waiting for the issues to arise before finding an answer is a dangerous approach that could, in certain instances it can result in a delay.

People who are highly reactive tend to react upon stimuli in a way that is not thought of and trigger an action-reaction mechanism. Although , in some instances, this method is effective particularly when time is limited, most of the time the triggered reaction lead us to commit more errors.

The prevention and insurance

Insurance companies attach a value to our possessions so that, in the event of an accident it is possible to recover their value. This outlook on the future is about avoiding certain scenarios and in preparing yourself to ensure that you don't lose everything.

The attitude of the insurer is thought to be as preventive. Be prepared for what could occur. Although being prepared is a good thing but it can also have negative aspects. For instance, fear could cause us to plan that everything is at a premium even though the odds of the possibility of a negative happening are tiny.

The conspiracy and the proactivity

They are constantly on their watch. Every signal can lead them to speculate and create complex plots that are, when compared with reality appear to be exaggerated. The conspiracy's view of the future is viewed as active and is based on taking action prior to something happening.

In the past it is evident that this approach adds greater than everybody else. As opposed to the preventive approach which is based on trying to avoid losing all of your possessions, the proactive approach is one that tries to alter the future. Make an effort to make sure that reality is able to adapt to our ideas. It's through the search of a particular future and is doing everything to achieve it.

After having analyzed the various approaches in the face of the future, it's normal to gravitate toward the two last ones which is the protection of the insurance company or the proactive supervision that of the conspiracy. That is, to take a stance that is geared towards anticipating the potential threats and opportunities which are ahead to help us correct our path, but not needing to abandon the course.

Chapter 15: Yoga And Mindfulness Meditation

Yoga

Yoga is a body and mind exercise. Yoga practice is delivered through an array of postures that improve flexibility, balance and quality as well as focusing. The postures that incorporate deep, breaths are great for:

Balance the backbone

improve mental clarity

Repair the sensorimotor system.

reduce depression and stress

can bring calm and emotional wellbeing

Yoga poses can be an enjoyable exercise for people suffering from anxiety or depression, and the most important part of this is breathing.

The breathing method used in yoga, like Ujjayi can reduce anxiety response framework and aids in achieving in achieving a calm and peaceful mind. It results in a mind-body connection that has a wide impact.

There are certain yoga poses which are particularly beneficial but a coordinated, general yoga practice meditation can help you reconnect with your real essence and the wholeness of your being. In this moment of Being there is the emergence that connects us to stressors and issues, motives for anxiety, or even the situations.

Here are some postures which can help specifically with depression:

Forward fold forward (Uttanasana) Yoga expert says about Uttanasana, "Any depression felt in the mind can be released If one is able to hold the position for two or more minutes."

Forward Bend Head-to-Knee (Janu Sirsasana) This slack forward fold poses is soothing your mind. It stretches the hamstrings, crotch and hamstrings, and stimulates the liver.

d kidneys.

Cobra (Bhujangasana) The Cobra (Bhujangasana) backbend is a possibility at a slower pace. It expands the midsection and allows for flexibility for the lungs.

span (Setu Bandha Sarvangasana) - The posture of extension is a backbend which strengthens the legs, widens the chest/midsection, and enlarges your stomach's organs and lungs and thyroid. The slender, held for a long time, and finished with a piece that is placed under your sacrum, can be an eating-related adaptation.

A headstand that is supported (Salamba Sirsasana) Sirsasana is referred to for being the "king of all postures". Inversions really change your body and provide your cerebrum cells a fresh source of blood.

Concentration and meditation are essential in this posture , and consequently it is a great way to clear your thoughts and restore your perspective. The various variations of sirsasana that can be and accompanied by props are additional alternatives.

Mindfulness Meditation

Guided meditation is a form of meditation in which you visualize a vision as much detail as you are able to. The system makes use of the power in positive speculation assist you in attain something particular as well as the feeling of happiness at the moment of happiness.

Mindful meditation is a way of life that allows you to focus completely on the present moment. Your thoughts, feelings and experiences are acknowledged without judgement. The benefits of caring are transformative mentally and physically, in your professional and personal connections, as well as your acceptance and understanding of yourself.

In Buddhist idea, our brains are referred to as "monkey personality "(PRIMAL). As monkeys shriek and scream as they move from tree to tree the brains of ours also scream and babble away, moving from thought to thought in the thought process.

Meditation helps you manage the noise and control your thoughts. This is accomplished by focusing on the present while letting go of your feelings and thoughts as they occur.

Mindful meditation is different from various forms of meditation as it involves focusing on the present moment. It is about letting go of all unnatural should-have, might-have contemplation. Instead, you live the moment with total acceptance. It is possible to attain this through meditation as well as daily life.

Be aware of your lifestyle habits

Many people who are depressed may also be troubled by alcohol or other substances. In addition to the fact that alcohol and drugs affect your mind and sleep patterns, but also with inspiration as well as reduce the effectiveness of your depression medicines.

Drinks and other food items with juices can cause nervousness and make it difficult to rest at night. Eliminating juice or a solid or hard daily perk-ups can assist in revealing signs of better sleep.

Seniors are more likely to suffer from the throes of depression. Based on the research those who suffer from depression tend to build in weight. Experts believe that the link between depression and weight. This could be because of changes in the body that occur in the immune capacity and hormones associated with depression.

Running for a good time is probably not on your mind when all is completed, you'll be miserable. may make leaving the house an exhausting task. If it's an exercise that is able to do wonderful things to one's mood and self-esteem and self-esteem, it's more beneficial.

It is important to take some time to relax especially if you're recovering from depression. If you just attempt to manage it your day when you're not able to concentrate your attention on the issue, then you'll provide yourself a tremendous favor. People who exercise regularly are less stressed.

Set up specific times throughout the day when you can deliberately relax and adhere to the timetable. It is possible to record these time slots in your everyday diary. You could also plan for your time off at work, perhaps having a break in order to attempt for a short walk.

Don't be afraid to ask for help from others you. For instance, determine if you can find a close family member or friend who will be able to take care of your youngsters for 60 minutes. Make sure to spend that time on your own needs.

Take a piece of fruit and examine it close and take note of the surface composition. Do you notice any modifications in the surface in the event you put it in light? Place it on your nose.

What is it like?

Eat the oranges and apples. In the first couple of bites, focus on the aroma, surface and the flavor. Which muscles of your body are being used? How does it feel to gulp?

As you practice mindfulness awareness/meditation, you will start to try to bring it into your natural life. Try to be "in this moment" each and every moment of the day, regardless of the situation you are in.

It is extremely effective in relieving depression and anxiety. This is vital since our bodies are designed to manage stress during emergencies however, prolonged anxiety will affect your mental and physical health. Your entire body is influenced by anxiety, but you're most vulnerable to:

hypertension, coronary disease as well as stroke

discomfort from muscle pain, especially the shoulder, neck back, neck and shoulders

disturbances in your digestive system , as well as your deep sleep and cerebral pains

Mental issues, including sadness, depression, and anxiety

skin disorders, such as skin conditions like psoriasis, dermatitis or pimples that flare up

The benefits of meditation have been proven to be beneficial:

reduce stress

Help with memory

Enhance center to focus

Enhance passion and flexibility

Improve self-esteem and increase compassion

It is believed the human brain is one of our biggest weaknesses. larger amount of slaves to our brains than professionals. By practicing meditation you can rid your mind from negative thoughts, lower the stress level, and take on the responsibility of your life.

If you're stressed your body produces more of certain hormones, like cortisol. These hormones trigger organs beneath the skin to release higher levels of hormones.

The excess of hormones harmful to your health may be trapped inside hair follicles, along with the dead skin cells and foundation which can cause pimples.

Hair that is shiny and thick isn't just a part of your appearance It's also a sign of your overall health. Your hair is always in a state of transition.

It begins to grow during the dynamic elimination and then is triggered during sleep. When you're intent on it the settling stage, your hair is in the settling stage for longer and you'll lose hair more quickly.

It might likewise be a sign for physical contact, for instance, an embrace or consoling hand set on an arm, and touch has been connected with helping depression-reduction.

A variety of methods can aid people in getting over anxiety or difficult situations.

Chapter 16: The topic is Conflict Management

As of now, you've learnt to distinguish your feelings from your rational and to be able to empathize with other people. These two strategies will only get us to the point of no return. It is now time to think about ways we can bring these skills together and utilize them to handle conflicts. Conflict management is a crucial capability to have, particularly in a work environment. The ability to manage conflict is among the most crucial assets of effective leadership.

* Re-evaluate your position. Before you begin to present your suggestions for a path to move forward you should take a moment to evaluate whether, after all the new information presented your position is the same. With the new data, it's essential to review your decision. It doesn't mean you're not right or that you're likely to need to alter your direction

however it does indicate that you're weighing all options. If you're in need of additional time to consider the new information and views be sure to let it be known and allow this time. It will earn you more respect than simply tearing your way through without weighing.

* Be results driven. In any setting there will be conflict at various stages. It's an inherent part of human nature. The most important thing to remember is that not every conflict is harmful and that when properly managed conflicts can boost productivity and creativity. That's why we approach this from the viewpoint of management, not just resolution. If conflict occurs You now have the ability to analyze the situation clinically, and calmly while simultaneously, you have been able to increase your sensitivity levels to the point that you can relate to others. It is at this stage where you've understood the various opinions that you must attempt to influence the result. This outcome will be

based upon the results you have now considered to be the most appropriate.

After having absorbed all the information provided and you might or might not have changed your mind however, you should have a clear understanding of what you would like to attain. Do not undervalue the importance of this step , or you'll be a bit sloppy in your answers. The people you interact with must see you being a person of power and having an idea of the direction you're heading. They may have thoughts that differ to yours but when you perform with confidence and focus, you're in a good position to obtain the outcome you'd like. Be aware that you are fully aware of your position, while they might not be able to fully grasp yours.

- Look for collaborative solutions. If you are able to comprehend all sides of the argument you're in a good position to express your objectives however, in a manner which includes all the arguments that conflict with your positions as you can. It isn't always the case every time, and we need to learn to recognize when there is overlap with our position as well as which aspects of the other's view can be considered valid for the outcome we are seeking. If someone else has given an opinion that is relevant and valid, don't dismiss it out from a lack of determination. Instead, you should try to find ways to integrate it into your solution. Credit when credit is due, and make it clear that the portion of the solution comes borrowed from someone else. This will strengthen their commitment to your cause more than they would otherwise.

Be clear in your arguments. To achieve your goal and avoid conflicts, the way you conduct yourself in this moment is crucial. Be clear about the outcome you want to achieve, but summarize the argument which others may have advocated, so it's clear you have considered their viewpoint into consideration. The majority of people, once they realize that their views are being considered and listened to they will change their mind when confronted by a different perspective. If you've presented your argument in a calm and rational manner and proved that you have a thorough understanding of the divergent opinions well There are three possible outcomes. The first is that they'll take your side since it is clearly superior. The other is that they'll accept your opinion because it's at least similar to their own , however you have stated it better. The third possibility is that they get stuck in their heels because they do not have developed their emotional intelligence to the degree that they can ignore a conflict of opinion, without having to get their personal way.

• Dealing with stubborn people. If you're forced to confront anyone who has allowed their emotional stance to overrule their rationality It is important to be cautious. One way to do this is to stick to the questions and assertions of fact. Certain facts are difficult to challenge. They are the most vile enemies of the emotionally dogmatic since they reveal the person's beliefs and lack of logical thinking. They tend to be very weak in emotional intelligence, yet they can also be most loud and opinionated. In a quiet way, confronting them with facts that can't be disproved at times but not always makes them feel less threatening.

* Be ready to leave. It's not a good decision to confront people who aren't prepared to let logic rule their thoughts, especially in a social setting. Instead, after thinking logically and calmly expressing yourself with clearly stated facts and inquiries and then step away from the possibility of confrontation. In a group setting, your reasoning will have been scrutinized and you will not make your case stronger by being caught up in a debate that you already won. Request a timeout, and hope your common sense can assert its own logic once the other is calmer or let someone else be the ones to lead the discussion and convince you. The bottom line is that what you're looking for is a win-win-win-win-win-win-win-win- the

Holy Grail may not be accomplished in the first try.

* You won't take on every challenge. After a long and hard work on the emotional intelligence of your character, it might be difficult to accept the fact that you may not always get your way, even when your logic suggests that you're right, and you've mastered every skill described in this guide. Remember that winning battles with grace is an integral part of a bigger battle and you are building the foundation that will hold you well in the long haul. What you're currently trying to do is making yourself known as a stable, emotional stable and clear thinking person. This includes understanding the fact that your emotional intelligence a process of development and occasionally you may be required to surrender to circumstances that are not logical or smart. It is important to have confidence in your capabilities that you know they will prevail at the end.

Chapter 17: The Habits To Develop To Ensure Success

It is said that those who succeed are the ordinary people who are able to develop extraordinary behaviors.

Many people are led to believe that success is the result of some talent that only a handful of individuals were fortunate enough to be born with, however it's not the case.

Everyone knows someone or more who has achieved success however they are unable to comprehend why they are so successful. They then ask whether it's due to one of the many possible reasons including the right behaviors. It could happen, however the mere existence of positive habits could not suffice to ensure your success. You must be careful about negative practices, too.

The majority of people think about the possibility of becoming extremely successful. What they fail to grasp is that everything they require to be successful is already inside them.

The reason certain people are able to attain the level of success they enjoy today is due to the habits they've created. These habits form around 95% of a person's behaviour. What you've been able to accomplish and what you're going to accomplish in the future will depend on the kind of habits you've been able to establish.

If you're able to establish good habits and to make positive changes then you'll succeed in your life and will be successful.

People who fail do not necessarily lack capabilities; it is that they're proficient in not achieving failure by sticking to bad routines. As time passes it is the way of life of a person that determine the likelihood that he/she will be likely to succeed.

It's a good fact that habits are learned habits, similar to other attributes that can be learned like cooking or driving. As with these abilities, your ability to improve your other habits will determine if you'll enjoy a fulfilling life.

A habit can be described to be "a established or regular habit or habit, and especially one that is difficult to break." This implies that you have a habit that you do every day as well as, like lacing up your shoes, it's something you do without needing to make an enormous amount of mental effort.

Making a ton of calls such as this, for instance, can be considered an habit however, if you're miserable while you're making those calls, then it's not really a habit and you'd be able to swap it to do something different.

This means that when it comes to the habits of one's life, it's not just something that you perform every day it is something that is now a part of your routine. This is why forming and understanding your habits could be quite difficult for a large portion of people.

Be goal-oriented

If you want to be successful One of the most important practices you need to develop is to develop a goal-orientated mindset. It is essential to learn to become an established goal-setting habit and then set your mind to writing down specific objectives every single day throughout your life. It is important to make the process of forming daily routines a habit yourself too.

The majority of people who are thought of as highly successful are extremely determined. They know what they wish to accomplish and write it down. They also plan out how they will attain their goals and they make plans, too. Every day they check their plans, and make sure that their plans are the basis of their daily routine.

Be driven by results

The goal is established with anticipation of the outcome which is the reason the most successful people are also driven by results. To be a result-driven person, you must adopt these two principles:

* Make it your the highest priority to constantly be learning something new to ensure that you improve your job.

Time management is crucial that is the second thing you should be doing. Time management can help you make your priorities for your tasks clearly. It can help you focus your attention on those things that are important. So, you'll be able to make the most of your time wisely.

In order to be truly successful, you need to concentrate on being results-driven.

Get Motivated to Take Action

For you to be successful you must develop the habit of consistently doing something. This is among the most essential habits to build if you want to establish a routine for success. Being action-oriented requires you to be skilled of always having an urge to act and maintaining a zeal to take actions. You must maintain the speed of your work in each project you are required to complete in order to reach your objectives. One of the worst behaviors to avoid is to delay your work. You must set aside your worries and do your best to accomplish your goals.

The ability to blend goals, results orientation with action orientation, is an excellent method for anyone who wants to succeed as it's a certain chance to succeed. You can also reference your SMART goals to identify the realistic targets which you can easily monitor and evaluate.

Be People-Oriented

The way people interact is also an essential aspect to achieve success. This practice allows you to build relationships that will be at the core of your existence. They are your choice to make and requires an effort to be kind, patient and compassionate. Your happiness and comfort in living your life depend on the way you manage to interact and connect with other people.

Fortunately, human beings have the ability to improve themselves and become better human beings when dealing with other people, however it requires a decision to do better in order to accomplish this.

According to Aristotle The best method to master an habit is to continue working on the habit. If you are looking to become an exceptional person, then you should begin by learning how to become a superior person in the way that you interact with others. Through practice, you'll begin to learn these traits and eventually you'll become the person you want to be.

It is also possible to create a new lifestyle built on positive thought by being at ease with the people you encounter during the daily running in your daily life.

Take care of your health

Being healthy is an additional tip to be successful It requires an enormous amount of effort. You must be vigilant about what you consume and make sure that you're on the right diet. Keep in mind that healthy eating does not mean that you must consume large portions of food. It means that you need to consume healthy food in proper proportions.

Exercise is also vital for health, which is why it is essential to do regular intervals by working all your muscles as well as all joints of your body to stay fit and alert. The most essential ways to ensure you are following a healthy lifestyle to be healthy is to get enough sleep.

The combination of recreation, appropriate diet and exercises, will allow you to go through life and in a healthy way. Remember how healthy you are the most crucial factor in your success and it is dependent on the habits you've developed in your daily routine.

Be Honest

The value of honesty and integrity can't be overemphasized. In the end all the behaviors you've managed to establish over through your life are more valuable than virtually everything else.

To be truthful You must adopt your "reality principle" in all of your dealings. When you conduct your business it is essential to be sure to remain honest with yourself and others as well as with the world around you. With specific values and rules for yourself, you'll be able organize your life and continue living your life according to your individual principles. Never compromise your integrity and peace to the benefit of anyone else , or for anything else in particular.

Being honest is crucial in determining if you will get into the other good habits you're trying to build.

Learn to be self-disciplined

Being disciplined and self-motivated is a habit that can guarantee the success of maintaining other habits.

Being able to manage and master yourself to manage your behavior is an important trait that, when considered in alone, can assist you grow as a person. This behavior is a key factor in achievement in all areas that you live in.

Be open to other opinions and constructive criticism

Positive feedback is an vital element in increasing the morale of a person. It can also provide an important source of motivation to aid you in attaining the success you desire. If you can accept constructive criticism and be encouraged to achieve your goals.

This is the kind of feedback that helps you become aware of areas in which you can improve, since it doesn't just inform you of your best areas as a person. When you receive constructive critique, you'll be aware of your flaws, and through training and personal/collective growth it will be possible to build yourself up to be healthier and more stable than you ever were.

You must be committed to achieving something Everyday

While it's always beneficial to get up with a positive outlook and energy, or to drive by taking action and maintaining positive attitudes however, it is not enough when you're not able to sustain this kind of enthusiasm throughout the day. If you are determined to succeed then you must adhere to your routines and determination to achieve your goals, or else you'll get distracted by the demands and the demands of the world.

While this means the fact that you possess a high amount of determination and strength in your character, this type of determination will give you the determination you require to support your pursuit of success over the duration of.

Do More Work That Your Competitors and the Others around you

When you are pursuing your objectives The only thing you will be in control of is the effort you put into along with your own actions. However, you must also remember that your personal success is contingent on the other people who surround you.

If you're competing against other people for a particular reward or for a particular objective, you're required to do all you can, and not take chances to achieve the goal. The key to success is your commitment to getting to your goal. You must be determined to do more than anyone else in the race to achieve the same goal with you. Prepare yourself to sacrifice things they normally wouldn't want to sacrifice.

Don't give in to complacency

One thing that stand between you and your achievement is complacency. This is a factor that could quickly manifest after you receive positive feedback, or even after you have reached your short-term objectives.

Instead of being satisfied instead, use these achievements or compliments as motivation for your motivation by making a commitment towards your objectives. The most successful athletes on the planet are those who never abandon their pursuits even when they have achieved their goals. They keep pushing their limits and set new goals for themselves. The majority of them will adhere to new fitness routines to increase their results.

Never be afraid of anyone Other than yourself

It's always difficult to strive for the success you desire in your job or work One reason for this is because you could at times meet with individuals who appear to be intimidating, yet they're also focused, who are working tirelessly to accomplish their goals. They'll always be present and you should not allow them to make you feel less than your abilities or devalue you as they will make you feel less than and may make you feel uncomfortable when faced with the competition.

Although it is crucial that you respect the other people who are with you as well as those within your circle, it is essential that you do not surrender to fear. Always work to improve your skills and aim for the success you desire.

Each of the behaviors which have been discussed in this section are the habits that most people have naturally and, even for those who don't already have these habits, they are ones which can be easily developed and utilized to maximize your potential.

The only reason you're where you're at and what you are now is due to the habits you've developed throughout your life. The majority the habits you have developed were created by you because of your experiences throughout your life as a child, from the time of infancy until the present day.

You now have the power to take control of your life and creating your character and character. If you're able to accomplish this, everything else that happens to you occur to you will be in the right direction because of your good choices that you've taken. The only thing you have to do is discover the right behaviors that will lead you to the desired success.

You can also look to successful individuals as a model for developing your own healthy ways of living. This will allow you to enjoy the successes they've achieved. Your possibilities are endless If you are willing to make the right choices.

Chapter 18: Being Aware of your emotions

Everyone has feelings We cry, we smile, get upset, sad and even confused. No matter what the circumstance there is always a kind of emotion. People who are suffering from "alexithymia" (a very rare mental illness) do not feel emotions. They don't know, recognize or express their feelings. They are rare and tend to be more common in males than females. If you're an alexithymic person, in this chapter we will examine ways to be more conscious of your feelings.

What are your feelings?

There has been plenty of discussion over the definition of feeling and the distinction between emotions and feelings.

Feelings Your personal perception of emotion or feeling. The subjective nature of feelings means that they cannot be proved or proven. They're less clear than emotions.

Moods: This describes your state of mind at a specific period of. It is the summation of your thoughts and feelings and lasts longer than an emotion.

Emotions They are an objective method of looking at the emotions. These emotions can be clearly clearly defined, and felt by all. Whatever your situation, whether you're experiencing an array of feelings, psychologists are able to discern the emotions and address them appropriately.

The way we feel is what makes us human. Being able to experience feelings of happiness, joy sorrow, sadness and excitement, as well as hurt and loss is what makes us human. The modern society was created to force us to lose out on the power to feel overwhelmed by work, school as well as our social lives.

A balanced state of mind helps you cope with difficult times and allows you to live a happier life. When you experience an imbalance in your emotions and feelings, you are less enthusiastic and anxious. For example, if you are aware that you will be taking an important test to take this week, then you likely have plans to study for the test. Some individuals like to remain up late to soak to absorb as much information as they can prior to the test (not advised) Some prefer to study in advance in order to get up early the night before to be alert and rested at the time of the exam.

How are you feeling?

The emotions are internal feelings However, they also create visible indicators. If you pay attention to these signals that you begin to recognize the emotions that are behind these signs. First, you need to begin paying attention to your arousal- the changes in your body associated with emotions. Different emotional states lead into different degrees of Arousal.

Certain emotions trigger alarms inside your mind. They instruct your brain how to set your body for swift actions in response to an attack. Let's take an example: you're walking along the sidewalk by yourself when you spot three gang members heading towards you. The gang members are seen as threats, and you are scared. While you're feeling fearful the brain informs your body to prepare for the event that you must take on or escape.

The body uses the fuel reserves for an instant burst of energy. The rate of breathing increases. Your body gets the oxygen it needs to utilize the fuel to fuel energy production. The heart rate increases, as well. This is a way to get more blood that contains oxygen and fuel to the places that you require it, including your brain and muscles. In the meantime your muscles get tense as you prepare for the next move. Anger and fear are two emotions which lead to high levels of arousal.

This is why you might feel the need to hit people when you're angry, or run away from the room when you're afraid. However sadness is a state of mind which causes feelings of low arousal. Instead running or fighting it's more as if you're slipping into a cocoon when you're down. Other emotions are somewhere between. If, for instance, you're angry, you might feel a little snappy. When you're stressed or anxious, you could feel a bit nervous. If you're content you might feel like jumping up and down

It would be extremely useful If Sign X always indicated that you felt Emotion Y. But, the reality isn't as easy. The same body sign can indicate different things in various situations. For instance, crying typically is associated with sadness. But, some people cry out of relief or out of sheer happiness. There aren't any strict guidelines, but there are general guidelines. These are a few of the physical signs that are often associated with certain emotions.

A more relaxed and joyful heartbeat
Feeling warm, laughing and smiling

The muscles that are tense and fear-inducing change in breathing Feeling cold sweating

Anger, faster heartbeats, tense muscles changes in breathing or feeling hot, shouting

The heart beat is faster, the muscles are tense and cold sensations crying, lump in throat

Certain of these symptoms are triggered by body temperature. You might not have considered the link between body temperature and emotions. It is likely, however, that you were at the very least cognizant of its connection.

The body signs that are listed above are good rule of the thumb. Each person has their own method of reacting to your emotions, but. A good way to find out more about this is through observation. If you experience a moment of overwhelmed, fearful, happy or sad, consider asking yourself what changes in your body you observe. If you're confused by the way you feel, your bodily reactions will help you figure things out. For instance, let's say the adorable student sitting right next to you in your math class has with you over a chat. Most of the time, you are content about this. However, you're also aware that your hands are becoming sweaty. Based on previous experiences you are aware that you're feeling nervous as well. This can, in turn, tip off: This could be the perfect time to take some deep, relaxing breaths.

DEEP DRILLING INSIDE your thoughts

When you look at the word "emotion but you're not aware of the emotion you're experiencing. If you do know that you're feeling uncomfortable regarding something, it might not be able to help you manage the feeling. It is possible to gain a greater understanding of the reasons you experience like you do in certain situations or with certain people or under certain conditions through analyzing your actions as well as your body's responses and those of other people's.

Did you make expressions or displayed anger and regret later? Our emotions can be very powerful and affect the way we interact with others as well as how much money is spent, the way we cope when faced with problems, and the way we use our time.

Controlling your emotions can help you grow mentally. The best part is that everyone can get more adept at controlling their emotions. Similar to the other skills, controlling your emotions is a matter of commitment and training.

If you experience negative emotions, take a moment to take a moment to slow down and pay consideration to how you feel and why you're feeling in the way you do.

Don't be afraid to acknowledge negative emotions, but don't be stuck in them too.

The ability to manage your emotions isn't the same thing as putting them down.

Doing nothing to alleviate your grief or pretending that you don't feel pain will not let those feelings go away. Instead, it gets worse over time. There's also a great chance that the act of suppressing your emotions could lead you to resort to unhealthy methods of coping such as alcohol or food.

It is essential to acknowledge your emotions and recognize that your emotions don't have to dictate your behavior. If you awake in the wrong place the bed, it is possible to be in control of your mood and change your outlook. If you're feeling unhappy, you can decide to be calm. If you're unhappy, you can make yourself feel happy. Be aware of those discomforting feelings However, you shouldn't let yourself get stuck in them. You deserve better.

POSITIVE emotions PEOPLE with high emotional intelligence POSSESS

There is a broad range of positive emotions that individuals who have high emotional intelligence can experience and aren't only restricted to the emotions listed below. They include:

Joy - the feeling of contentment, excitement and happiness that are present when something happens that is good

The feeling of gratitude is appreciation for the work accomplished, and is usually accompanied by humility and respect.

Serenity is a peaceful and calm feeling of acceptance for oneself and of the surrounding.

A sensation of curiosity or fascination that catches the attention of a person.

Hope is a hope and optimism for a positive future.

A feeling of self-esteem for a feat, talent or personal quality.

Amusement is a satisfaction that is a feeling of happiness and satisfaction, frequently accompanied with laughter and smiles.

An inspiration - feeling of excitement, joy and inspiration by something emotional that you have witnessed.

Awe - it is felt when you see something magnificent extraordinary, amazing, or stunning that creates a feeling of profound admiration.

Elevation occurs when you witness someone in acts of kindness or openness, or goodness. It then inspires you to emulate them.

Altruism - it is known as self-sacrifice and generosity toward others. However, it can be seen when you assist others.

Satisfaction is a feeling of fulfillment and pleasure you feel by doing something or satisfying the need.

The sensation of joy that you feel when a difficult situation changes into something positive

Affection is an emotional bond with an individual or thing that is accompanied by similarity and enjoyment in their relationship.

A feeling of happiness, feeling positive, and feeling that everything will turn out for you.

The feeling of surprise is a feeling of delight when someone offers something completely unexpected that makes you feel happy.

Confidence is a feeling that comes from the feeling of self-worth, and faith in one's abilities.

Admiration - the sense of reverence and appreciation to someone or something.

Enthusiasm: A feeling of excitement that is followed by inspiration and commitment.

The feeling of eagerness is the state of being ready and excitement about some thing or person.

Euphoria - a feeling of joy or exuberance that is experienced when something satisfying and exciting occurs.

Contentment is an optimistic, calm feeling of happiness and wellbeing.

Feeling of enjoyment - it's a feeling of being enthralled in the world within you.

Positive outlook - this is a positive and optimistic emotion that makes you think of a bright and bright future.

Happiness - it's an emotion of joy and satisfaction with how things are going

The emotion of love is the most intense of positive emotions. It's the sensation of long-lasting and deep love towards the person you love.

Understanding the emotions of others

Social intelligence refers to a person's ability to understand how others are feeling and, in a certain degree managing the behavior and emotions of the individuals. If you prefer to be on your own, then you don't be concerned about how others think or feel.

Nobody is an island Therefore, you need to be able to communicate regularly with others and, with a keen sense of social you can create more efficient interactions. If you can understand what people are feeling, then you will be able to;

Maintain good relations

Help a person gain confidence to feel confident about yourself

Do a favor for someone and not make them feel like they are being used.

Sell an idea or product to an individual

Help a person to be calm

Help others when they are in need.

Find a group of your family and friends who can engage in mutually enjoyable activities with.

When you interact with people there is no need to be a huge giver to achieve the outcome you desire. Being aware of your surroundings and managing your own feelings can be very beneficial.

It's not just all about pleasing others. It's also about being able to discern other people's perspectives and apply your emotions appropriately. Therefore, in certain situations emotional intelligence can mean that you have to be tough with someone else or tell them that you're not satisfied. Emotional intelligence refers to being capable of understanding and reading the other person's perspective and use your emotions appropriately.

EXAMINING self-destructive BEHAVIORS

Consider some of the most harmful habits including smoking, drinking too much or consuming drugs. A lot of people have developed smoking cigarettes to create a sense of stylish, elegant or social. The first sensation you feel when you puff or hold on cigarettes (even even if the experience isn't pleasant) will make you keep smoking. Your feelings or sensations about your self (looking and feeling good) will lead you to adopt an habit to smoke. In some cases, fear or anxiety can take the best of them and they begin smoking. The majority of people begin smoking due to peer pressure.

What if more of us identify these triggers (emotions which trigger an action) prior to the time they begin smoking. Recognizing these trigger feelings and understanding the reason why they're occurring can open the way for a new set of behaviours or habits. A number of smokers have confessed their feelings, and even knew what they were feeling and had the option to quit smoking cigarettes or not, they'd choose smoking. Though this knowledge may aid some new smokers not to smoke, or at the very least lead to making a better informed choice however, being aware of trigger feelings does not necessarily mean that you're done smoking.

Conclusion

Emotional intelligence can be used to help you achieve success. If you don't have the components of emotional intelligence , such as self-awareness, self-control, and confidence in oneself, the path towards success could be difficult to navigate.

Insufficiency in emotional intelligence can cause stress and negativity to swathe over you in a flash of rage. If you lack the ability to manage your emotions, you may lose your friends, financial status relationships, and even yourself too. It is crucial to manage your moods and behavior.

The stability of your emotions is the main requirement for a positive development of the human. It can be achieved by taking a honest self-assessment each time. To develop, we must improve and evolve. It's not that we have to change our character and take on the personality of the neighbor across the street. It is simply that we need to learn to correct our negative behaviour as well as no one is able to influence our moods unless we empower them achieve this.

Understanding oneself is the top goal. Only when we are conscious of how we'll react to certain situations can we be self-confident and confident in ourselves. Individuals must be able to trust ourselves. For as long as we're living, it is our responsibility to be feeling and be emotionally. There will never be an era where we could say that we don't feel anything. While feeling nothing, we are as if we're numb. It is essential to accept the fact that we are human and accept it.

Feelings shared with others makes one realize that they are not the only one. When others relate to our sadness and emotions We realize that it is a part of our human nature. However, we must be careful about the way we express our emotions. The act of storing emotions in our minds is dangerous. Consider the illustration of the hot coal. If you hold it in your hands it could cause you to suffer burning pain, but if you let it go and let it go, it won't hurt you. It is the same with emotions. It is essential to let them go before they hurt us inside. Remaining in the dark about our feelings could cause severe stress, depression, and sadness.

Lailah Gifty once said that endure pain and uncomfortable situations isn't simple. It is easier to give up and forget about the discomfort. But, if you do give up, you'll suffer further. It is better to bear the pain today and be able to enjoy the life you have later. It is all about endurance.

www.ingramcontent.com/pod-product-compliance
Lightning Source LLC
Chambersburg PA
CBHW071837080526
44589CB00012B/1021